THE BEST OF
SICKIPEDIA

Compiled by

Ivor Hugh Jardon

Spelling, punctuation and grammar checked by

Fles - "It's all about clause and effect!"

Cover design, formatting and editing by

Esby

Published by

Sickipedia

Copyright © 2014 by Sickipedia

D1439861

DISCLAIMER

The content of this book is packed full of inappropriate material. It is definitely **NOT** suitable for children or the easily offended. Within these pages are jokes about religion, racism, crime and illegal sex acts. Remember: what you read are not points of view, they are jokes - nothing more!

Every effort has been made to try to ensure that the pages of this volume contain no jokes by professional comedians. Please be assured that if any have slipped through the net then it was an entirely unintended oversight and accept our unreserved apologies for this.

Thanks to all the members that helped make this book possible.

Sickipedia.org

"Sorting the wit from the chavs"

Contents

Introduction

What you hold in your hands is a collection of the sickest, most depraved and bloody funniest jokes from the pages of Sickipedia.org. Does that make you sick and depraved? Afraid so but, given the number of people who visit our little corner of the internet to create, share, and read such filth, you are part of a large community.

Genuinely though, we would like to thank the community at Sickipedia (or Sickipedians as they are better known) as, without them, none of this would have been possible. All of the jokes and content that you will see in this book have come from their sick and twisted minds - and we wouldn't have them any other way! Also, by claiming that they are the providers of the filth that follows, it gets us of the hook legally.

Now why on earth are you still reading this? The jokes start on the next page. Go on, get the fuck away with you!

Some Top Jokes

A man goes into a library and asks for a book on suicide.

The librarian says, "Fuck off, you won't bring it back."

A man was walking his dog through the graveyard when he saw another man crouching behind a gravestone.

"Morning!" he said.

The other man replied, "No, just having a shit."

So here I am in the Internet Cafe with the biggest fucking nigger I've ever seen reading every word I ty

---

This morning on the way to work, I drove into the back of a car at some lights whilst not really paying attention.

The driver got out and he was a dwarf.

He said, "I'm not happy."

I replied, "Well, which one are you then?"

Statistically 9/11 Americans won't get this.

What's black and doesn't work?

Half of London.

A woman brings eight-year-old Johnny home and tells his mother that he was caught playing doctors and nurses with Mary, her eight-year-old daughter.

Johnny's mother says, "Let's not be too harsh on them... they are bound to be curious about sex at that age."

"Curious about sex?" replies Mary's mother. "He's taken her fucking appendix out!"

I'm not racist.

Racism is a crime and crime is for black people.

What do you do if you come across a tiger in the jungle?

Wipe it off and apologise.

I'm American, and I'm sick of people saying America is "the stupidest country in the world."

Personally, I think Europe is the stupidest country in the world.

You know you're on Sickipedia too much when you start learning the news from the jokes.

An elderly British gentleman of 83 arrived in Paris by plane.

At the French immigration desk, the man took a few minutes to locate his passport in his carry-on bag.

"You have been to France before, Monsieur?" the Immigration officer asked, sarcastically.

The elderly gentleman admitted he had been to France previously.

"Then you should know well enough to have your passport ready."

The British gentleman says, "The last time I was here, I didn't have to show it."

"Impossible. The British always have to show their passports on arrival in France!"

The elderly gentleman gave the French Immigration Officer a long, hard look.

Then he quietly explained:

"Well, the last time I was here, I came ashore on Juno Beach on D-Day in June 1944, and I couldn't find any fucking Frenchmen to show it to."

My cousin's a lazy bastard - sits around all day doing fuck all, drinking and surfing the internet for porn.

Jeez, I wish I had an office job too!

Why don't black people go on cruises?

They're not falling for that one again.

A pub landlord is shutting up for the night when there is a knock at the door. When he answers, a tramp asks him for a tooth-pick. He gives him the toothpick and the tramp goes off.

A few minutes later there is a second knock. When he answers, there is a second tramp who also asks for a toothpick. He gets his toothpick and off he goes.

There is a third knock at the door, and a third tramp. The landlord says, "Don't tell me, you want a toothpick too."

"No, a straw," says the tramp.

The landlord gives him a straw but is curious as to why he wants it, so he asks the tramp why he wants a straw and not a toothpick.

To which the tramp replies, "Some bloke just threw up outside but all the good stuff's gone already."

This girl told me that she wouldn't sleep with me if I was the last person on Earth.

If I was the last person on Earth, she wouldn't have a choice in the matter.

I was chatting to an American about all the pain we felt on 9/11/2001. I should know - I caught my foreskin in my zip that day.

Which, by the way, was the 9th of November.

Christianity: One woman's lie about having an affair that got seriously out of hand.

My wife, being unhappy with my mood swings, bought me one of those mood rings so she could monitor my mood.

We discovered that when I am in a good mood, it turns green and when I am in a bad mood, it leaves a big fucking red mark on her forehead.

I just had an argument with a girl I know. She was saying how it's unfair that if a guy fucks a different girl every week, he's a legend, but if a girl fucks just two guys in a year, she's a slut.

So, in response, I told her that if a key opens lots of locks then it's a master key, but if a lock is opened by lots of keys then it's a shitty lock.

That shut her up.

A black man takes a girl home from a nightclub.

She says, "Show me it's true what they say about black men."

So he stabs her and nicks her purse.

What do you do when your dishwasher stops working?

Punch her in the face.

Have you heard the joke about the baby with AIDS?

It never gets old.

The other day I needed to pay a visit to the toilet, and I found a public toilet that had two cubicles.

One of the doors was locked. So I went into the other one, closed the door, dropped my trousers and sat down.

A voice came from the cubicle next to me: "Hello, mate, how are you doing?"

Although I thought that it was a bit strange, I didn't want to be rude, so I replied, "Not too bad, thanks."

After a short pause, I heard the voice again. "So, what are you up to?"

Again I answered, somewhat reluctantly, "Just having a quick shit... How about yourself?"

The next thing I heard him say was, "Sorry, mate, I'll have to call you back. I've got some cunt in the cubicle next to me answering everything I say."

I had my first sexual experience at infants' school: I shagged little Jenny Jenkins behind the bike sheds.

She said I was better at fucking than I was at teaching maths.

A family are driving behind a garbage truck when a dildo flies out and thumps against the windscreen.

Embarrassed, and to spare her young son's innocence, the mother turns around and says, "Don't worry, that was an insect."

To which her son replies, "I'm surprised it could get off the ground with a cock like that."

The other day I told my neighbour Jerome that he was like Marmite.

He said, "What, you either love me or you hate me?"

I said, "No, you're black and you smell."

Just had a water fight over the park with a bunch of local kids.

I won!

No-one's a match for me and my kettle.

Some random woman stopped me in the street today and started telling me a joke. It had all the ingredients of a good joke: child abuse, incestual rape, tears and suffering. But I didn't understand the punchline.

Something about £2 a month?

I'm going to go rob a bank tomorrow.

I plan on dressing-up in a clown wig and make-up and only wearing a thong and nipple tassels.

I'll carry a goat and a can of fluorescent paint in one arm and, while in the bank, I'm going to fuck the goat and throw the paint over the walls, all the time ripping up pages of a phonebook and swearing my head off. After getting the money, I'll take a shit on the floor and piss everywhere. I then will escape in a van shaped like a giant pink cock.

Let's see Crimewatch fucking stage a reconstruction of that!

Two Serbian soldiers are holed up guarding a hilltop. After a while, Pieter tells his buddy he is off for a shit, and he heads off looking for a bush.

After twenty minutes, Dimitri starts getting worried, as Pieter still has not returned. Time continues to pass, and, more and more, Dimitri fears his comrade-in-arms has been killed.

After an hour, Dimitri decides to get on the radio and is just about to call for a unit to search for his fellow soldier when Pieter appears, bold as brass, with a huge grin on his face.

Dimitri: "Pieter! Fucking hell, I thought you were dead! Where have you been?"

Pieter: "Well I went off to find a bush to take a shit in and, when I found one, I was crouching down and I saw this beautiful Croatian bitch: gorgeous tits, legs to die for. So, I finish my shit and I go over and start fondling her tits. I stick my finger in her cunt, then I take out my cock and I fuck her hard, then I come on her tits. After that, I roll her over and fuck her again in the arse, then I roll her over again and I come again all over her tits!"

Dmitri: "Did she then suck the last of your come from your cock?"

Pieter: "Don't be a fucking idiot! Her head had been blown off by a grenade!"

The new barman in the pub is black, so I said to him, "Beer please, nigger."

He hit the roof and said, "Why don't we swap places? Let's see how you like it!"

So I went round behind the bar; he walked out, then came back in and said, "Beer please, honkey."

I said, "Sorry mate, we don't serve niggers in here."

The Sickipedia 10 Commandments:

1. Thou shalt not worship any sites but Sickipedia.

2. Thou shalt not take the name of Sickipedia into work, or polite company.

3. Honour your original author.

4. Thou shalt not dupe.

5. Thou shalt not steal jokes from Mock the Week.

6. Thou shalt not steal jokes for Facebook or Twitter without crediting the author.

7. Thou shalt bear breasts upon the forum.

8. Thou shalt not commit adultery, but write jokes detailing how bad thy wife is.

9. Thou shalt check your fucking spelling before you upload a joke or post in the forums.

10. Thou shalt not break virgins in on the Sabbath.

Crime - The Police

Fifteen skinheads chased a Pakistani into a shop and proceed to kick seven flavours of shit out of him. Eventually, the police arrived and arrested everyone.

One of the coppers walked over to the shop assistant and asked if he saw it all happen.

When the clerk replied, "Yes," the cop asked why he didn't help out.

"I thought fifteen was enough," came the reply.

What do you call a policewoman who shaves her pubes?

Cuntstubble

West Midlands police are looking for a "racist attacker".

I phoned the information line but apparently it's not a job advertisement!

My wife said to me, "I've just heard some great news, apparently the police know who the local paedophile is and they are going to arrest him tonight."

I said, "That's brilliant news. Let's celebrate by moving to Australia."

A Paki has been run over by a reversing car.

Police are appealing for the driver to come forward.

A bloke is driving happily along in his car with his girlfriend when he's pulled over by the police. The police officer approaches him and asks, "Have you been drinking, sir?"

"No," replies the man. "Why, was I all over the road?"

"Not at all," replies the officer, "You were driving splendidly. It was the ugly fat bird in the passenger seat that made me suspicious."

A bloke at work was jailed last week after police found videos on his mobile of a girl being raped.

Serves him right for stealing my phone.

Two Irishmen are walking past a Police Station. A big poster at the front reads "Two black men wanted for rape!"

Paddy turns to Mick and says, "Dem fokkers always get the best jobs".

The Metropolitan Police have said they are looking for a black man in his twenties.

And always will be.

After extensive investigations and many phone calls, the police found that, despite the fact that I'm black, I've got a good job, no criminal record and I own the BMW I was driving.

So they arrested me for wasting police time.

Threw a penny down a well today and made a wish:

"I wish the police don't look for Penny down this well."

A black police officer stopped me in the street today.

"Up against the wall," he snapped. "Now, empty your pockets."

"Wait a minute, I'm confused," I replied. "Am I being arrested or robbed?"

I was stumbling down the road having had a skin-full after work when a police car pulled up beside me.

"What are you up to?" asked the policeman.

"I'm off to the Paki shop to abuse the cunt and give him a slap," I slurred.

"Talk like that gets you a ride in this cop car, lad. So get in the back now...

...he shuts in five minutes and you won't make it in time on foot."

Police raided Katie Price's home and found a man in her bedroom.

They arrested him for loitering in a public place.

The police knocked on my door this evening.

"Where were you around 8:05 last night, sir?" asked the officer.

"Funny you should ask," I replied. "I took the wife upstairs at 8 pm to make love."

"That's true," my wife shouted over, "but fuck knows where he was at five past."

What has six legs and a cunt on the middle of its back?

A Police horse.

I went for a job interview with the police. I thought I'd blown the observation test when they'd played this graphic video with two coppers giving this Pakistani a right pasting. It was so violent that I winced and dropped my coffee.

"Now, what can you tell me about what you've seen?" asked the Inspector.

"I'm really sorry but nothing much at all because I was cleaning up the coffee."

"Good lad! You've got the job."

Whilst I was driving, my girlfriend started giving me a blowjob.

I thought I would give her a quick lick as well but I ended up crashing.

The police have charged me with doing 69 in a 30 zone.

The police kicked my door in last week and dragged me out of the house. They told my wife that I was wanted for male rape.

To be fair, they let me go the next day, but my arse was so battered that I couldn't sit down for a week.

Our young daughter had been missing for several hours and my wife was starting to become frantic.

We called the police and they began to organise a search of the surrounding area. The police sergeant told us they were bringing in a sniffer dog to help.

"Do you have a sample of her clothes?" asked the officer. So, I handed him a pair of my daughter's panties.

He sniffed at the underwear and began slobbering, excited by the scent.

"But officer," I said, "shouldn't we wait for the dog to arrive?"

Crime - Sex Crimes

Rape - If you don't ask, she can't say no.

I asked a group of women if they found rape jokes funny. They said, "No!"

But I knew they really meant "Yes."

Rape is a strong word.

Not according to Hotmail when I try to use it as a password for my account.

My daughter was distraught after being attacked and raped walking home from the pub.

I put my arm around her to comfort her. "You need to take more care," I told her. "Tonight it was me, but tomorrow it could be a complete stranger."

My wife got raped on the way back from the chip shop earlier and was rushed straight to hospital. I was devastated when I found out.

I was really looking forward to those chips.

I hate having to walk through parks alone at night.

Makes me wonder why I became a rapist in the first place.

A very polite young man brought my semi-conscious daughter home early last night.

"I can only apologise sir," he said, "But someone appears to have spiked Claire's drink."

I thought, 'What kind of twat does a thing like that?'

He could have fucked her and she'd have never remembered anything.

I took a girl home from the pub last night and fucked her. Then I made her sleep in the wet patch.

It was only fair, they were her tears.

"Buy some lucky heather, mister?" asked this cute little gypsy girl.

"Nah, you've got loads and it's definitely not that lucky!" I replied.

"What makes you say that?" she grinned.

"Well, you're about to get raped, love."

Only a coward would use Rohypnol to rape a poor girl.

Real men wear masks.

For me, having sex is a lot like spreading butter on toast.

It's possible with a credit card, but so much easier with a knife.

I was in hospital the other day when I saw a sign that read "Rape Victims."

So I did.

I would have gotten away with it if it wasn't for those meddling kids!

And the large amount of semen found at the crime scene.

Necrophilia - putting the rot in erotic.

The BBC are commissioning a new forensic crime series focussing on finding evidence of necrophilia from the corpse.

It's called "Wanking the Dead."

I caught my dad bumming my mum earlier.

That was bad enough, worse when you consider that my mum died last month.

What separates rape and necrophilia?

About an hour.

Remember: it's not necrophilia if she's on life support!

My girlfriend recently broke up with me after rejecting the idea that we have sex in a graveyard.

I'm not too upset though, she'll die eventually.

Smile and the whole world smiles with you.

Doesn't work if you're standing over a dead child, covered in her blood, with your pants around your ankles.

I found a young homeless girl hidden out by the bins last night. She was dirty and didn't smell too good but, underneath the grime, I could see she was pretty and had a good body.

I brought her inside and gave her a bath. As I was towelling off her naked body, I became aroused and one thing led to another. Before I knew it, I was making passionate love to her.

I was banging her so hard that a couple of times, you'd have sworn she was alive.

What do necrophilia and January have in common?

They're both fucking cold.

Paedophilia - it's just childish.

I was raping a woman the other night and she cried, "Please, think of my children!"

Kinky bitch.

Didn't help myself in court yesterday.

I was arrested for child porn charges and the Judge said, "How does 5-6 years sound?"

I said, "Sexy."

Paedophiles are fucking immature arseholes.

Women are like squaring numbers.

If they are under 13, just do them in your head.

Like most 16 year old girls my age,

I'm a 42 year old man.

They say a picture is worth a thousand words.

The pictures on my computer are worth a long sentence.

Me and my mate like to rate girls out of ten.

The best thing is, to passers-by it just sounds like we're trying to guess their age.

I'm not one of those guys who disappears right after sex.

I like to spend some time with them afterwards, have a bit of a cuddle, stroke their hair and make it absolutely clear what I'll do to them if they tell their parents.

I was at a party at the weekend and, after a few drinks, I took a girl upstairs to one of the bedrooms.

Just as I was pulling her knickers off with my teeth, the door opened.

I said, "Do you fucking mind? We're a bit busy here"

Then a little voice said, "Daddy, mummy's looking for you. It's time to do my candles"

I have fond memories of playing kiss chase at school.

As a teacher, I was always faster and stronger than the kids.

What do you call a disabled paedophile?

A creepy crawly.

I was looking for a new flat and found a nice place in the centre of town that seemed ideal.

"It's only £600 a month," the woman told me. "But no children or pets."

I had to turn it down. It was a bargain, but I wasn't willing to give up my sex life.

My paedophilia is starting to become a serious problem – it's taking over my life.

Last night I had a wank, then had another one over my sperm.

What's the difference between a nipple and a cock?

Nothing, according to my new born son.

Life is a lot like my penis.

Harder with kids.

What's the worst thing about paedophilia?

No titty wanks.

A Scottish paedophile has raised a dispute with eBay.

He claims the Wii Game Boy he received isn't what he was expecting.

I burst into a hotel I was passing with a young girl over my shoulder last night.

"Please, I've just found her unconscious in the street," I panted. "I think she's taken an overdose of drugs."

"Shall I phone an ambulance?" the receptionist panicked.

"No!" I replied. "I want a room."

My neighbours just found out that I'm on the sex offenders list and have demanded that I move out of the area as they fear that I am a danger to their son.

Their son? I'm a paedophile, I'm not gay!

My fiancée left me after a small misunderstanding.

She asked if I ever fancied having children.

I said, "Actually, there is one in particular I've had my eye on…"

I can't believe I got my computer seized just for having Virgin Media.

Or, as the police like to call it, 'child pornography'.

Crime - Drink & Drugs

"Sir, could you please step out of the vehicle?"

"I'm too drunk, you get in."

A policewoman arrested a man for drunk driving.

The female officer tells the man, "Sir, you have the right to remain silent. Anything you say can and will be held against you."

"Great idea!" the drunk replies. "Tits!"

I can't believe that I got arrested the other night for speeding in a 30mph zone.

I was only going at 32mph or 33mph - I'm not quite sure which one it was though, I was pretty drunk at the time.

I got arrested for being drunk and disorderly last night and the officer told me:

"I've already notified your wife sir"

"And what did she say?"

"Nothing"

"Bollocks, that's not my wife!"

My mate died after taking an E.

Countdown's security staff don't fuck about.

The police raided my flat this morning and arrested me for growing cannabis.

Thank fuck for that, I thought they were after my laptop.

A police officer is parked outside a bar one night when he sees a drunk man stumble out of the door. The man staggers through the parking lot and falls down. He tries his keys in five different cars before getting in one and driving off. The cop immediately pulls him over and makes the man take a breathalyser test. The man blows a 0.0.

"This thing must be broken," the cop says.

The man responds, "Nope, tonight I'm the designated decoy!"

I got arrested for being drunk and disorderly. The policewoman asked me to come quietly...

...which brought me a separate charge.

Drugs and alcohol are never the answer.

Unless someone asks me, "What are you doing this weekend?"

I persuaded my girlfriend to smuggle my coke through customs by sticking it up her arse.

I didn't know I could buy another can in the departure lounge.

Following an amputation, the black guy at the end of my street only has one hand.

He's dealing with it.

People say that marijuana is good for you because it's natural, but they don't realise that just because it's natural, it doesn't mean it is safe. Want to know what else is natural?

Bears.

On leaving a club with a girl, I slipped something into her drink which will guarantee me a dirty night in bed.

Laxatives.

When my wife asked me if I was high, I just laughed.

Uncontrollably.

For fifteen minutes.

Crime - Theft

What is the difference between Batman and a black man?

Batman can go into a convenience store without Robin.

Harry is visiting his grandma. She complains about the high cost of living. "When I was a girl, you could go out with a shilling and come back home with a dozen eggs, two pints of milk, a pound of bacon, half a pound of tea and a fresh chicken."

"Yes," says Harry, "that's inflation for you."

"It's nothing to do with inflation," says grandma. "It's all them fucking CCTV cameras they have nowadays."

I stole the punctuation keys from a Judge's PC recently.

I'm expecting a long sentence.

A bank robber walks up to one of his hostages and asks, "Did you see my face?"

The hostage replies, "Yes."

The robber takes aim and shoots the man in the head.

He turns to the next man. "And did you see my face?"

"No, but my wife caught a glimpse!"

Everybody says stealing is wrong.

Personally, I don't buy it.

My grandad always said, "Don't watch your money; watch your health." So one day, while I was watching my health, someone stole my money.

It was my grandad.

My mate called round earlier. "I didn't know you had a dog," he said.

"Yeah, we got him about a week ago. Poor little sod had been abandoned."

"Abandoned?" he said. "Who'd abandon a friendly little fella like him?"

"Makes you wonder, doesn't it?" I replied. "Some cruel bastard had just left him tied to a post outside the supermarket."

I found an iPhone on the bus today, so I called the number in the contacts that said 'Home'.

"Hello!" I said when they answered. "I've found your phone on the bus."

"Oh, that's fantastic!" the woman sighed with relief.

"I know it is," I replied. "How do I work the camera?"

It was bloody cold this morning in Liverpool. I went out to the car and it was minus four.

Minus four fucking wheels! Bastards!

My grandad came to visit today.

Before he arrived, I said to my young son, "Whatever you do, don't mention the war."

He said, "Why, will it bring back terrible memories?"

I said, "Nah, I took the old cunt's medals down to Cash Converters this morning."

The recession has got so bad, I've had to resort to crime.

I've got a striped pullover, a Lone Ranger mask, a beret, and a bag with "SWAG" written on it.

At least if anyone sees me, they won't be taken seriously by the police.

Wife: "Chris! Wake up Chris, I think I heard someone downstairs. Go and check it out for me."

Husband: "What? Why do I have to go and check?"

Wife: "Because you're the man of the house and you always brag about how tough you are! Now go and prove it, for God's sake!"

Husband: "Well, I'm not going. So you're going to have to do it yourself."

Wife: "Chris! What about the children!?"

Husband: "That's a brilliant idea! Which one should we send?"

Crime - Murder

"I've got a new nickname for you," I told my wife today.

"What is it?" she asked.

"Bambi," I replied.

"Aww, is that 'cos I've got beautiful eyes?" she asked.

"No, it's because I've just killed your mum," I replied.

My son will soon be getting to that age where he acts like my cat.

He'll start bringing birds home in such poor condition, I'll have to take them into the backyard and kill them with a brick.

As my wife lay dead on the floor, the weapon next to her, the detective said, "Do you want to tell me what happened?"

"I was cleaning it and it went off," I replied.

"It's a fucking bow and arrow!" he shouted.

My wife is always complaining that I don't know how to clean up properly.

Thirty rapes, five murders, and not one single arrest states otherwise.

My wife and I took our family on holiday, but when we were on the plane we realised that we had forgotten our son.

While we were away two burglars tried to rob the house. It was just like that film Home Alone.

Except they raped and murdered him.

As I crushed the painkillers and poured them into a glass of vodka, I looked at a picture of my wife. "We'll be together soon, my darling," I said.

"Did you say something?" my wife asked from the next room.

"I'm on the phone to your sister," I said. "Your drink is ready, by the way."

I was walking the dog in the park earlier.

Ended up raping and murdering an old woman.

I'm only kidding.

I don't have a dog.

My grandfather developed cancer when he was younger.

Some say he's the most evil scientist who ever lived.

After three years of marriage, me and the wife had our first real fight last night.

I called my dad for advice on how to fix things.

He told me to apologise and admit I was wrong.

I was really looking for advice on how to dispose of the body.

Everyone in my village has been out searching for a missing little girl, so I thought I'd go round and console the girl's mother.

"Don't worry," I said, "I'm sure she'll turn up soon."

"Oh," she wept, "do you really think so?"

"Oh yes," I replied. "All the farmers start ploughing this week."

Crime - Other Crimes

"Kidnapping" is a strong word.

I prefer to think of it as "surprise adoption."

I've just been chatting to my neighbour's teenage daughter and it turns out she's really into UFOs and aliens.

Which is cool, because tomorrow she's getting abducted.

I was in the house the other day when I thought I heard my daughter, in the garden, screaming about being kidnapped.

Must've been my imagination though - when I checked the garden she wasn't there.

My ten-year-old daughter has just set up a Facebook account.

I said to her, "Choose your profile picture carefully."

"Why's that, Dad?" she asked.

"Because it'll be the one they use when you go missing."

Apparently, someone in London gets stabbed every 52 seconds.

Poor bastard.

My little girl has spent all day whining about how hard her life is.

"You should count yourself lucky!" I said. "You come from a good home with loving parents."

"I know," she said with a tear in her eye. "Will I ever see them again?"

I finally think I've reached the point in my life where I'm ready for kids now.

I've passed my driving test and bought a transit van.

A lady walks into a Gun Shop and asks for help in choosing a rifle. "It's for my husband," she says.

"Did he say what calibre he wanted?" the assistant asked.

The lady replied, "You must be joking - he doesn't even know I'm going to shoot him!"

My wife said to me today, "Did you know that hippopotamuses kill more people every year than guns?"

"Yes", I replied, "but a gun is easier to conceal."

This is yet to be confirmed by scientists, but there are rumours that women have a certain 'spot', and if you hit this spot at exactly the right strength, it will make a woman willing to do anything for you.

It's called the face.

Did you hear about the lonely pyromaniac?

He's still looking for the perfect match.

My wife wears the trousers in my house.

They cover up the bruises from the previous night's savage and unprovoked beating.

'Why do you always burn my food?' I asked my wife for the hundredth time.

'Oh, stop fucking moaning,' she said. 'I can't be bothered with all that cooking shit, so I wait till the smoke alarm goes off and then I know it'll be done.'

So, after she put the chip pan on tonight, I turned the heat on full, took the batteries out of the alarm and fucked off down the pub for my alibi.

This angry looking copper just came up to me and said, "Give me your name."

I said, "Why, what's wrong with yours?"

What Not to Say on a First Date

"Christ, my bollocks are itchy."

"Does this look infected to you?"

"Yeah, you'll do until something better comes along."

"How the fuck did you fit into those jeans?"

"My mum got rid of hers with Immac."

"Ever go on Sickipedia?"

"Sorry, I thought we were supposed to meet naked."

"Hope you brought your purse, fatty, we're going Dutch."

"You don't, by any chance, happen to have any Mace in your purse, do you love?"

"Get under the table, my wife's just walked in."

"I hope you don't mind, I brought my son with me. Pay no attention, he's got Tourette's."

"You have a disabled son? I know how you feel, my telly's been broke for weeks."

"Can you help me with this ointment? I have a stubborn rash that just won't leave."

"I didn't think I was rehabilitated, but that's the cutbacks for you."

"You have something on your chin. No, the other one!"

"What's with the wig? You on chemo or something?"

"When you gonna start your diet, then?"

"Vaginal intercourse is so outdated, don't you agree?"

"This is a lovely French restaurant, don't you think? I took my ex here once. She had frogs legs and chicken breasts, but she had a great personality."

"You get the drinks in, I'm going for a shit."

"Mmm... why, yes, I love to have my toes sucked. I find that saliva really soothes the fungal itching."

"I thought this would be weird because I fucked your mum, but it really isn't."

"Open your legs, please. I need to check you're not a man."

"That seat's taken, fatty. I'm waiting for my blind date."

"I bet you'd fuck like a demon... with being a slapper and all."

"Don't worry about condoms, love. I can't catch anything else."

"What are you having, Rohypnol and Coke?"

Illness and Mortality - Cancer

My wife is forever saying I don't pay her any attention. So yesterday I was expecting brownie points when I said, "Have you had your hair done, dear? You look different."

She went ballistic. I won't forget she's having chemotherapy again in a hurry.

A woman visits her doctor complaining of a strange feeling in her lower stomach. The doctor examines her and states, "Well, I can tell you that you'll need to be buying lots of nappies in about nine months' time."

"Am I pregnant? That's wonderful news!"

"No, you have bowel cancer."

When my wife found out she had breast cancer, I handed her a box of tissues.

She said, "I'm not going to cry."

I said, "I know, but you'll need them for padding."

The woman in the local cancer charity shop has just called me an inconsiderate bitch for smoking outside her window.

I told her to fuck off. If it wasn't for people like me, she'd be out of a job.

I was in the queue in Tesco and the woman in front was joined by her mum with another basket of shopping.

"Fuck's sake," I muttered under my breath. "Take all day, why don't you?"

She turned on me. "If that's all you have to worry about, I feel sorry for you. I'm dying of cancer, you know!"

"In that case," I snapped, "you of all people should understand the need to get a fucking move on."

I was in the pub last night when my wife texted me:

Hi Darling, I've just opened my letter from the hospital about my lump.

Do you want to know the results? xxx

I texted back:

No, please don't tell me.

I'll watch Match of the Day when I get in. xxx

My missus has just completed 'Race for Life'.

I was so moved by the whole event, I decided to set up my own charity race for males suffering with testicular cancer.

Unfortunately I had to cancel the event after receiving complaints from the council and residents.

Apparently 'Run Your Bollocks Off' is not an acceptable name.

The Doctor drew the curtains around my hospital bed.

"I'm afraid it's bad news, Mr Evans," he said. "The tumour is inoperable... You have only weeks to live."

"I'm not bothered," I nonchalantly replied.

He looked at me curiously, "May I ask why not?"

"Certainly. My name's Foster. Mr Evans is in the bed opposite."

I am pissed off with my wife. I love her big tits, but she has gone in to hospital for a breast reduction.

I've told her, I would prefer her to keep her breast and die of the cancer.

I've just found out my girlfriend has terminal cancer and the doctor has given her less than nine months to live.

On the upside, at least I don't have to worry about getting her pregnant now.

After seeing all the advice regarding self-examinations for testicular cancer, I decided to give it a go. Sadly I actually found a lump next to my right bollock.

It turned out to be my left bollock.

I went to see my doctor today.

He said, "I'm afraid you have cancer."

"Well at least I won't have to get my hair cut anymore," I replied, looking for positives from the situation.

"True," he nodded. "You'll be dead in a few days."

My wife had been suffering from crippling stomach pains for a couple of days, so I advised her to go to the doctor.

When she returned and told me she was HIV positive, I was absolutely devastated.

I had a brilliant cancer joke lined up.

Illness and Mortality - AIDS & STDs

One of my ex-girlfriends phoned me today to say that she's just discovered she's HIV positive.

She was very upset and apologetic, and stressed that I get tested immediately in case I've also been infected.

I had a long chat with her and managed to calm her down in the end.

I told her there was no need for me to be tested, as I was already diagnosed with it at a young age.

So, I've just been diagnosed with HIV. My doctor has advised me to remain positive.

I can't see how that's going to help.

My girlfriend's got so many genital warts...

When I cum over her fanny, it looks like a bowl of Rice Krispies.

TV advert: Just £2 will give aid to an African child.

I thought they were born with it.

I asked my girlfriend for a blow job today and she replied with, "Well, what will I get?"

I'm guessing Herpes was not the right answer.

I can tell when someone's lying pretty easily.

Last Saturday, I was raping a woman and she screamed at me: "The fucking joke's on you, you cunt! I'm HIV positive!"

I shrugged and said with a smile, "What a coincidence, so am I," and continued.

That changed her fucking tune.

Gay Ray goes into the doctor's office and has some tests run.

The doctor comes back and says, "Ray, I'm not going to beat around the bush, you have AIDS."

Ray is devastated. "Doc, what can I do?"

"Eat 1 curry sausage, 1 head of cabbage, 20 unpeeled carrots drenched in hot sauce, 10 jalapeno peppers, 40 walnuts and 40 peanuts, 1/2 box of grape nuts cereal, and top it off with a gallon of prune juice."

Ray asks bewildered, "Will that cure me, Doc?"

Doc says, "No, but it should leave you with a better understanding of what your fucking arse is for."

What's dangerous and eats nuts?

Syphilis.

A boy was in a science class learning about sexually transmitted infections.

The teacher said, "Now, there is nothing funny about syphilis."

The boy said, "There is if your doctor has a lisp."

I had unprotected sex with a girl on a one-night-stand last night.

Afterwards she said, "Wow! That was amazing. You never told me you had such a big dick."

I replied, "Cheers. It's not normally that big though... It's just very swollen at the moment because of the infection."

Apparently, STDs lower your sperm count and therefore reduce your chance of getting a girl pregnant.

Which is great for me because I hate condoms.

What have Chlamydia and a cheating husband got in common?

My wife has both of them and doesn't know about it yet.

---

1 in 6 women are said to have Chlamydia.

Well, I must be fucking unlucky because every woman I sleep with calls me up a few weeks later telling me she's got it.

I was shocked last night to learn my twelve-year-old sister has caught Chlamydia.

I didn't even know I had it!

Illness and Mortality - Dementia

"Knock-knock."

"Who's there?"

"Dave."

"Dave who?"

Dave holds back tears as he realises his mother's Alzheimer's is getting worse.

Roses are red.

Violets are blue.

I've got Alzheimer's.

This little piggy went to market.

Welcome to The Alzheimer's information web page.

Please enter your 16 digit password.

My uncle came out of the closet yesterday.

He's not gay.

He has Alzheimer's and thought it was the car.

It has been revealed that the latest research shows more money is now spent on boob jobs and Viagra than on Alzheimer's research.

This means that by 2040, the elderly will all have perky tits and stiff cocks, but absolutely no idea why.

A guy takes his wife to the Doctor.

The Doc says, "Well, it's either Alzheimer's disease or Aids."

"What do you mean?" The guy says, "You can't tell the difference?"

"Yeah, the two look a lot alike in the early stages. Tell you what, drive her way out into the country, kick her out of the car and, if she finds her way back home, don't fuck her."

"You can't touch that!" I shouted.

"Why the fuck not?" came the reply.

"Because you're fucking black, you cunt!"

Chess has become so frustrating since my old man got Alzheimer's.

My wife getting Alzheimer's has really spiced up our sex life.

You never know when a sex session will turn into a rape.

Want to hear my joke about constipation and dementia?

Tough shit, I've forgotten it!

When I was a kid, I was molested by my grandfather who had Alzheimer's.

It was terrible. Half way through he'd forget what he was doing and I'd have to finish myself off.

Illness and Mortality - Disabilities

After nearly breaking my neck on a pair of bright pink roller skates on the stairs, I shouted at my son, "Are these yours?!"

He said, "Well, obviously they're not mine."

"Oh yeah, of course they aren't," I replied.

Then laughed at him in his little wheelchair.

I think it's about time we stop making fun of people in wheelchairs.

I mean just put yourselves in their shoes.

Those clean, un-scuffed shoes, which some might even say look as though they haven't even been worn-in.

My daughter came home today wearing a new dress.

She did a spin and asked how she looked.

"Fantastic," I said. "You hardly notice the wheelchair at all."

It took a lot of balls for me to go on the Channel 4 show "Embarrassing Bodies".

Three, actually.

I organised a day of sponsored bungee jumping for the local disabled children.

Perhaps calling it 'Spastics on Elastic' wasn't my finest hour.

So I've got a new girlfriend.

She invited me round to her place for dinner the other night.

We were in the kitchen, just about to start making dinner, when she asked me to turn on the veg.

Apparently fingering her paraplegic daughter was not the right move.

I've just got back from my mate Dave's house where I met his brother, Tony, who is built like a brick shit-house.

On the flip-side of that, he's also retarded and, to demonstrate this, my mate told me he could tell Tony to do anything and he would do it.

With that Dave says, "Tony, piss yourself." And, believe it or not, he did just that.

"Shit," I exclaimed and suddenly, before my very eyes, this mammoth of a man began straining until he had indeed shat himself.

The next three words out of my mouth will haunt me for the rest of my life. "Well, fuck me!"

The voices in my head may not be real...

...but they have some fucking good ideas!

I saw a bloke let his dog walk straight out in front of a lorry this morning.

The cruel cunt didn't even flinch when it was killed. He was too busy standing there, trying to look cool in his sunglasses.

I'm very pissed off at my girlfriend. She got a new shirt today. It reads:

"Stop staring at my tits."

In Braille!

Why do buses have Braille on the stop button?

The blind bastards still can't see where their stop is!

A blind man is walking down the street with his guide dog when it leads him to smack into a post.

Once he's recovered, the blind man reaches into his pocket and fetches out a treat to feed the dog.

A passer-by remarks, "That's marvellous! Even after he's made a mistake like that, you're giving him a treat."

"Not really," says the blind man. "I'm just trying to find which end is which so I can kick him in the bollocks!"

A man walked into my shop with a dog on a lead.

I said, "You can't bring dogs in here."

He replied, "I'm blind and it's my guide dog."

I apologised and said, "Oh right, I see."

He replied, "Alright mate, don't rub it in."

My deaf girlfriend was talking in her sleep last night.

She nearly took my fucking eye out.

I never know what to say when I meet a deaf person. Then I realise...

I can say anything I fucking want.

My Jewish mate has been with his Tourette's suffering girlfriend for years now.

I always wondered what kept them together.

Then I saw the swear jar.

A man walks in to a library and asks for a book on Tourette's.

The librarian says, "Fuck off, you cunt."

The man says, "Yep, that's the one."

Old MacDonald had Tourette's. E-I-E-I-CUNT

"What's your name?"

"Colin Fucking Wilson."

"Do you suffer from Tourette's, Colin?"

"No, but the Vicar at my Christening did."

Did you hear about the leper who had a wank?

God knows how he pulled it off.

I knocked at my neighbour's door today.

"Your son has just run out in front of my car," I snapped. "I nearly killed him."

"I'm so sorry," she gasped. "He won't be doing it again."

"I know he won't," I replied. "The paramedic said that he was probably paralysed."

Illness and Mortality - Death

My 84 year old grandad was decorating our front room earlier and, unfortunately, whilst in the middle of doing so, his body gave up and he kicked the bucket.

The daft bastard got paint everywhere!

Have you ever noticed that it's only 'perfect' people who are murdered or killed in horrific accidents?

"He was the perfect son" or "She was the perfect daughter."

"Such a tragic accident, they were the perfect family."

"They died together, the perfect couple till the very end."

Makes me glad I abuse my kids and beat up my wife.

Kind of makes me immortal.

I was in Tesco yesterday when this woman dropped down dead in front of me.

She'd just bought a bag for life. Irony's a bitch.

On my tombstone I want it to say:

'I didn't forward the text message to 15 friends.'

When I die, I want to be thrown out of a plane wearing a Superman costume.

My grandad gave me some sound advice on his deathbed.

"It's worth spending money on good speakers," he told me.

I said to my wife, "Do you hear that? No one whining, moaning or complaining. The sound of silence. It's beautiful isn't it?"

And placed her urn back on the mantelpiece.

Little Johnny goes into school after being absent the previous day.

His teacher demands, "Where were you yesterday?"

"I'm sorry, Miss, my dad got burnt," replies Johnny.

"Oh, I'm sorry, I hope it wasn't serious," says the teacher.

To which Johnny replies, "Well, they don't fuck about at the crematorium, Miss."

My mother-in-law came in to work at lunch today and, I must admit, I was genuinely pleased to see her.

I'm an undertaker.

I popped my head over my sexy neighbour's fence today to see her lying in her bikini.

"Wow, you're gorgeous!" I burst out, "I hope you know how to do CPR."

"Why?" she asked with a giggle. "Because I've taken your breath away?"

"No," I replied. "I've just run your son over out front."

I dispute those studies that claim people often die from smoking.

My uncle smoked, and he only died once.

How very odd... Some girl has had all her Valentine's flowers and teddy bears delivered to a lamp post on the A12 near Brentwood this evening.

Judging by the amount there, she must be a right slag.

I refuse to go bungee jumping.

I came into this world because of a broken rubber and I don't want to leave it the same way.

A man once told his son that if he wanted to live a long life, the secret was to sprinkle a little gunpowder on his cornflakes every morning. The son did this religiously, and lived to be 93.

When he died, he left 6 children, 11 grandchildren, 27 great-grandchildren, and a 15-foot hole in the wall of the crematorium.

The Sickipedians Guide to Britishness:

1 It is a British custom to shut the fuck up on any train journey before 7AM.

2 It is a British custom to drink with your co-workers occasionally, even if they are cunts.

3 It is a British custom to wear clothing like jeans, trousers, a suit, or tracksuits; not fucking desert pajamas.

4 It is a British custom to accept a humorous jibe towards you, with the correct response being a humorous retort - not burning an effigy!

5 Anyone from Scotland/France/Germany/USA is a cunt.

6 Don't talk in the lift/at the urinal; which, in Manchester, are often taken to be the same place.

7 It is a British tradition to get bummed in fee-paying schools.

8 It's a British custom that, if your child marries the wrong person, you disown them not honour-kill them.

9 Tea is a drink, not a meal.

10 Beer is ale, not lager/cider/alcopops/shorts.

11 Football is played with feet, not hands.

12 When out with your mates, it is customary to wolf-whistle at a girl, no matter if she is hot or not.

Racism - The British

I'm getting sick and tired of all these immigrants coming to this country and working 100 hour weeks to set up successful business ventures that decent British folk could have set up, if only they had thought of them and had the drive and ambition to come off the dole.

What's the difference between a cow and a tragedy?

A Scouser probably wouldn't know how to milk a cow.

Liverpool airport has been shut for the past 8 hours due to a "suspicious car".

Apparently it had tax and insurance, and the radio was still in it.

Scousers take everything seriously.

No, seriously, they take everything!

A report out today says 60% of girls under 16 in Liverpool are binge-drinking on a regular basis.

I am shocked. Who the fuck is looking after their kids?

Most Scousers can trace their family tree back at least fifteen generations.

All the way back to 1980.

There has been a surge in the number of people jogging in Liverpool since a local health campaign claimed you would receive loads of new benefits if you started keeping fit.

I walked up to a black man in my store today who looked a little suspicious.

I said to him, "Could you empty your pockets, please."

"Are you accusing me of robbin' coz' I am black?" he asked.

"No," I replied, "because you've got a Liverpool top on."

Did you know that 100% of women from Liverpool carry an anti-rape alarm?

Their voice.

What's the difference between being born in London and born in Liverpool?

If you're born and live in London, you're a Londoner born 'n' bred.

If you're born and live in Liverpool, you're a Liverpudlian born inbred.

What do you get if you cross London with a bicycle?

Stabbed

"There's no such thing as can't"

Unless, of course, you're cockney; then you probably are one.

What does a cockney bird do with her cunt first thing in the morning?

Sends him to work.

I was walking along the road earlier and suddenly this horrid stench hit me. I presumed I'd stepped in dog shit so I looked at my shoes, but I couldn't see any. I carried on walking, and the smell got stronger and stronger. I just couldn't figure out why.

Then I realised what I'd stepped in.

Birmingham.

Suicide bombers have today attacked Bradford city centre.

Early estimates suggest they may have caused thousands of pounds worth of improvements.

More than 20 students have tested positive for TB at Manchester Metropolitan University.

A spokesman said these are the best results they've had in years.

What did one Geordie say to another Geordie?

Something incomprehensible.

The fact that there are Geordies in this world proves that, many years ago, a Scotsman climbed over Hadrian's Wall and raped a pig.

I've just seen a Norwich version of "Back to the Future". Unlike the original, Marty McFly can't resist the advances of his mother, so he ends up fucking her.

Then he travels back in time.

My mate from Norfolk has got ten perfectly formed fingers.

On his left foot.

Chessington World of Adventures today announced they are scrapping their family pass.

The whole of fucking Norfolk turned up, and got in for 36 quid.

Racism - Chavs, Pikeys and Gypsies

Why is a Chav's baseball cap like a clitoris?

Because it's above a cunt and under a hood.

What do you call a Chav in a suit?

A fucking cunt.

Don't let the suit fool you.

If you see 'Made in England' written on a product, you know that it is going to work.

Ironically, if you see a person with 'Made in England' tattooed on them, it's completely the opposite.

A police officer is driving down a quiet road when he sees a pregnant Chav girl with a coat hanger up her pussy.

Police officer says, "I'm arresting you on suspicion of performing an illegal abortion."

The Chav girl replies, "Nah mate, I'm just piercin' its ears, innit."

I've just got a job as a benefit fraud prevention officer.

I go around council estates kicking pregnant chavs in the stomach.

I just watched some Pikeys getting married on Gypsy Weddings.

The only possible reason I can see for the bride to have such an elaborate dress with so many layers is that, by the time her groom has peeled it off, she may be nearing the age of consent.

I've invented a new game.

You get a group of Pikeys and lock them in a cellar for a month without any food.

It's called 'Hungry Hungry Gyppos.'

The E.U. has decided that you are no longer allowed to use the word 'Pikey.'

You must now use the phrase 'Caravan Utilising Nomadic Traveller.'

Or CUNT for short.

A young pikey girl asks her mum, "Which way round do my knickers go on, Mum?"

Her mum replies, "How many fucking times do I have to tell ya? Yellow at the front and brown at the back."

I've decided to become a gypsy.

I don't like travelling, but I do like fifteen year old girls dressed like slags.

Racism - The Scottish

What's big, Scottish and depressing?

Scotland.

News: "Scots throw away £460 worth of food per person every year"

Maybe McDonald's should stop putting salad in their burgers.

I was walking through Glasgow today, when I was stopped by a representative from Aquafresh Toothpaste.

She said, "Did you know that the average person only brushes 30% of their teeth?"

I said, "We're in Glasgow, love: the average person only has 30% of their teeth."

Why do Scotsmen have blue willies?

Because they are tight fisted wankers.

Why is Andy Murray like Susan Boyle's vagina?

Both are useless Scottish cunts.

A petition for Scotland to be granted independence has attracted one million signatures.

And that's just from England.

Chilling statistics have revealed that weapons including meat cleavers and knuckle-dusters have been removed from Scottish schools.

One teacher said: "To be fair, we only ever use them in self-defence."

For my stag do, my best man said he was taking me where only the very tightest cunts in the country could be found.

Lidl in Glasgow.

In a Scottish classroom, the teacher asks a student, "If you have five pounds, and I ask you to lend me two, how many pounds do you have left?"

"Five."

A biker has been banned for hitting the fastest ever speed on a Scottish road - 166mph.

This beats the previous best of 158mph set by a Tennent's Super Lager delivery driver passing through Glasgow.

A bloke walks into a bar and orders a beer off the barman. The barman says, "That'll be 50p, please."

The man is amazed at the price, drinks his drink and then asks how much a cocktail costs.

"That's one pound, mate, for any cocktail."

The man then drinks a Pina Colada, feeling very pleased with himself. He then spots three men sitting in the corner looking miserable, and without any drinks, so he says to the barmen, "What are those men over there doing without drinks at this price?"

The barman replies, "They're Scottish. They're waiting for happy hour!"

Racism - The Welsh

An Englishman, Irishman and a Scotsman walk into a pub.

We didn't invite the Welshman because he's a cunt.

Gareth had a little lamb.

His father had it too.

If you're into bestiality,

Wales is the place for you.

Why can't Welsh people count sheep to help them get to sleep?

Because, when they get to five, they've got to stop and have a wank.

Welsh paedophiles.

Putting the 'Ddyfidd' into 'Kiddy fiddling'.

Did you hear the price of lamb in Wales has just gone up?

It's now £4.95 per hour.

Where else but Wales can you get a fuck, a nice warm coat AND a casserole all from the same date.

My wife made the allegation, "I think you've had an affair with that Welsh tart, from Llanfairpwllgwyngyllgogerychwyrndrobwllllantysil-iogogogoch."

I said, "How can you say such a thing?"

I was talking to a bloke down the pub earlier, and it turns out he'd lost his mother, father and sister all in the same week. Also his wife had left him, which means he has to travel from Cardiff to London every week just to see his kids, and on top of this, he'd been sacked from his job.

I felt so bad for him.

I mean, imagine coming from Wales.

England's relationship with Wales is based on trust and understanding.

They don't trust us and we don't understand them.

Dyslexic Welsh people: how would we know?

Racism - The Irish

Paddy phones EasyJet to book a flight.

"Certainly, sir," replies the assistant. "And how many will be flying with you, Mr O'Toole?"

Paddy replies, "How the fuck should I know? It's your plane!"

I was shopping in Ireland when I saw a man trying to cram a trolley into the boot of his car.

"I don't think you should be doing that, mate," I shouted.

He replied, "Are ye kiddin' me, lad? I paid a feckin' quid for 'dis!"

Paddy was asked why he kept an empty milk bottle in his fridge.

He said, "Dat's in case somebody wants derr coffee black!"

Paddy and Murphy are on a cruise ship.

Paddy says, "It's awfully quiet on deck tonight."

Murphy says, "Everyone will be watching the band."

Paddy says, "There isn't a band playing tonight."

So Murphy says, "I definitely heard someone say, 'a band on ship'."

Paddy takes his new wife home on his wedding night.

She lies on the bed, spread-eagled naked, and says, "Paddy, you know what I want?"

"Yeah! The whole fucking bed, by the looks of it!"

My Irish mate walked into the pub and said, "I'll have five bottles of your finest champagne!"

"Bloody hell," I said, "What are you splashing out for?"

"I won the jackpot," he smiled. "I got three numbers on the national lottery last night."

"You have to get six, Paddy," I said.

"Fuck it then," he shouted. "Six bottles of your finest champagne!"

I'm sick of all the Irish stereotypes.

As soon as I finish this drink, I'm punching someone.

Two Irish blokes walk into a pub.

"How many should we have this time?" asks the first one.

"Remember last time we were in here we had four and we didn't finish the last one."

"Don't worry, this time we'll get only three. Hey, barman, three bags of crisps and twenty pints of Guinness, please!"

The police were investigating an attempted rape case.

While interviewing the victim, it transpired that she believed the 'would-be' rapist was Irish.

"Did he have an Irish accent?"

"No, he didn't speak."

"Did he wear clothes that looked Irish, with shamrocks, harps or the like?"

"No, it was dark and I couldn't see."

"Well, what then?"

"He strapped my legs tightly together so I couldn't run away!"

Racism - Europe

I can't see the big deal with calling a Pakistani a Paki.

It's just the same as calling an Australian an Aussie, a Scotsman a Scot or a Frenchman a Cunt.

What's the difference between a French woman and a basketball team?

The basketball team showers after four periods.

Over 40,000 parasites and 250 bacteria are shared in a typical French kiss.

These figures are significantly lower in other countries, where people shower daily and don't eat snails or rotting cheese.

A French guest staying at a hotel in England phoned room service and asked for some pepper.

"Black pepper or white pepper?" asked the manager.

"Toilette pepper!" he replied.

I've just been arrested at Charles De Gaulle airport on suspicion of smuggling banned substances into France.

They found soap and deodorant in my hand luggage.

How do you know when a Frenchman has been in your garden?

All your bins are empty and your cat's pregnant.

What do you call a pointless race that covers 2,200 miles throughout France?

The French.

My mates were taking the piss out of a German guy on the train, making jokes about the War and stuff.

He looked at us and said, "You know, there really is no pleasure to be gained in boasting about winning two World Wars."

How the fuck would he know?

It's easy to see that Müller Corners are German.

The pure white part gets almost all the space and the rest is concentrated.

A German walks into a library and asks for a book on war.

The librarian replies, "No, mate, you'll lose it."

Some kid was playing up and being a right twat in Tesco, so his dad gave him a smack. This German woman came over, tapped the dad on the shoulder and said, "In my country we don't smack our children."

He replied, "Well, in our country we don't gas our Jews."

I was in Berlin last week in a pub, talking to the barman, when he asked: "Are you enjoying the city? It is one of the flattest in Europe."

I replied, "Is that because of the natural Geography or is it due to the RAF?"

Apparently that wasn't the answer he was looking for.

I've spent the day in a German police station. Word to the wise...

Don't go hailing a taxi in Germany like you do in Britain.

Tesco has announced 20,000 new jobs are to be created in the UK.

Poland's Prime Minister has welcomed the news.

I was with the wife in Tesco and saw polish remover.

Couldn't help thinking, "Finally, a solution for those bastards next door."

I walked out of the Job Centre last week after signing on.

Some guy across the road jeered, "Hey, you, you lazy cunt! How come you can't get a job, eh? I have two!"

I said, "I think you've just answered your own question there, you Polish bastard!"

What is long and hard that a Polish bride gets on her wedding night?

A new surname.

How many Spaniards does it take to change a light bulb?

Juan.

What's the difference between a Spaniard and a kipper?

One's brown, smelly and oily... and the other is a fish.

BBC NEWS: Spanish airport workers call off major strike.

Lazy Dago bastards couldn't even be bothered to do fuck all!

I thought Manual Labour was a Spanish waiter.

Then again, I though Hertz van Rental was a Dutch painter.

I've just got back from Amsterdam and, while I was there, I was sat in a cafe when I noticed a man coughing quite loudly, but I just ignored him.

He started coughing even louder, but I still just ignored him.

Eventually he began to cough and choke really badly, so I jumped up and smacked him really hard on the back.

Anyway, it turned out he was just speaking Dutch.

Racism - Americans

America: a country where people believe the moon landing was faked but wrestling is real.

How do you convince Americans to get involved in a war?

Tell them it's nearly finished.

Even though we both speak the same language, it's amazing how there are some subtle differences between American-English and proper English:

They say, "Sidewalk." We say, "Pavement."

They say, "Pants." We say, "Trousers."

They say, "Buried at sea." We say, "Naked and chained to a metal bed frame with a car battery connected to his bollocks whilst being beaten for answers."

I've just put a deposit down on a Porsche and mentioned it on Twitter.

I can't understand why the Americans are so upset.

All I said was, "I can't wait for the new 911."

I failed my history test today.

Apparently, "Three centuries of inbreeding," is not the correct answer to "How did the American people evolve?"

50% of Americans don't have a passport.

It's not that they don't want to leave their country...

They're just too fat to fit into a photo booth.

An American man moves to the U.K. to find some work. He manages to find a job in a bank.

On his first day, the boss tells him to sweep up the floor.

"Excuse me? I'm from one of the best colleges in the U.S.A.!"

"Oh, I'm so very sorry!" replied the bank manager, "Let me call someone in to show you how to do it."

How much does the average American have to eat, before he weighs 18 stone?

Fuck all for about 3 years should do the trick!

Recently, I saw an article about Americans sending their old clothes over to the poor in Africa.

Pointless! I've never seen an African with a 52 inch waist.

Racism - Asian

I had the Hiroshima Breakfast this morning.

One giant mushroom and loads of burnt soldiers

99% of Japanese are cremated, the highest rate worldwide.

It has remained popular since it was introduced to the country by the Americans in 1945.

Why are the Japanese afraid of Muslim women?

They think they're ninjas.

As a photographer, imagine my delight when I got a job to photograph pupils at a predominantly Chinese school.

I made a fortune, and only had to take one photo.

This Chinese chap goes into a bank to change some currency. After receiving his money he asks, "How come I came in here with same amount of money as yesterday but today I get less Yuans in return?"

The banker says, "Fluctuations."

The Chinese guy replies, "Fluck you Blitish too."

I saw this guy in an Italian restaurant ordering pizza in fluent Italian. The waiter seemed to appreciate his willingness to accept their culture.

So, I tried the same thing in our local Chinese restaurant.

I squinted my eyes and shouted, "Harro! Spesha frah raice, prease!" But, instead of showing appreciation, they took the upturned prawn-cracker basket from my head and told me to get out.

I saw a Chinese guy supping a pint in my local pub.

I said, "Excuse me, mate, do you know kung fu?"

He said, "Ha, vewy funny, iz 'cause I am Chinese man?"

I said, "No, you cunt, because you're drinking my pint."

A guy phones up a Chinese and says, "Do you do take-aways?"

The reply is, "Yes."

So he says, "What's 89 minus 14?"

Even though they asked politely, I told my Chinese neighbour's kids I'd walk the dog myself.

They'll only make a meal out of it.

I was recently asked about my views on euthanasia.

I said, "They all look the same to me."

I booked an Asian prostitute last night, but she arrived two hours late.

She loved me wrong time.

My friend suggested we go for noodles, but I told him that I have a big problem with those things you have to eat them with.

Asians.

Isn't it strange how words that sound the same have different meanings in different languages?

For instance, in the English speaking world "Sirens" are found on loud emergency vehicles, whereas in Japan it means "Be quiet."

Learn Chinese in 5 minutes:

Are you harbouring a fugitive? - Hu Yu Hai Ding

See me ASAP - Kum Hia

Stupid man - Dum Fuk

Small horse - Tai Ni Po Ni

Did you go to the beach? - Wai Yu So Tan

I bumped into the coffee table - Ai Bang Mai Fa Kin Ni

I think you need a facelift - Chin Tu Fat

It's dark in here - Wai So Dim

I thought you were on a diet - Wai Yu Mun Ching

This is a tow-away zone - No Pah King

Our meeting is next week - Wai Yu Kum Nao

Staying out of sight - Lei Ying Lo

He's cleaning his vehicle - Wa Shing Ka

Your body odour is offensive - Yu Stin Ki Pu

Great - Fa Kin Su Pah

Racism - Indians & Pakistanis

I failed my Politics exam. The question was: "Describe the role that India plays in the modern world."

Apparently "Tech Support" is not the correct answer.

My daughter is at Brownies tonight.

It's her first sleepover, so I hope Sinita's parents take good care of her.

Fuck me, directory enquiries must be mind readers.

I rang up for the number of a curry house and, judging by the accent on the other end of the line, they'd already put me through.

Barclay's are apparently "Fluent in Finance."

Well, that's fantastic. It's just a shame none of the fucking Indians that answer their phones are fluent in English.

When you take a White girl's virginity, you pop-her-cherry.

So by that logic, when you take an Indian girl's virginity, you pop-her-dom.

A gas explosion in a street in Bradford has killed 50 Pakistanis.

Rescuers are now searching a second house.

My wife told me I'm not allowed to call it "The Paki Shop" anymore, so we've compromised.

I now call it "The Newsasians".

What do you call a Paki with pink hair?

Gandhi floss.

What does a Paki girl dip into her tea?

Her moustache.

I saw a Paki drowning the other day and reported it to the Emergency Services.

I hope they saved him or that was a waste of a first class stamp.

If people from Pakistan want to be called Pakistanis they should rename their country Pakistanistan.

And stay there.

A consultant surgeon asks his colleague, "Have you informed the Paki in bed nine he only has a week to live?"

"Yes," he replies.

"Oh, you cunt! I wanted to tell him!"

The harbour police is on patrol on the Thames. Suddenly they see a small boat with two Pakis. They ask the two guys, "What are you doing?"

The Pakis answer, "We're going to invade London!"

"Hah, just the two of you?"

"No, we're the last ones. All the others are already there."

I put a job advert in the paper, but apparently you can't say, "No blacks or Pakis."

So I put the next best thing.

"Hard, honest worker with good hygiene required."

Apparently Pakis don't smell.

I think that's a Turban Myth.

Advice to any young men thinking about marrying a Pakistani girl.

If you want to know what she'll look like when she's forty, look at her father.

Racism - Black

How does every Black joke start?

By looking over your shoulder!

I got thrown out of a nightclub last night. This big black bouncer said to me, "Just go home."

Ironically, this was the exact same as my comment to him that got me thrown out.

When does a black man turn into a nigger?

As soon as he leaves the room.

I've always stood up for black people.

It's not worth getting stabbed over a seat.

After complaints that there aren't enough black people on British television, the BBC have vowed to solve the problem.

They are now going to show Crimewatch seven nights a week.

What's the difference between extortion and rape?

The spelling of blackmail.

I got chased by a nigger the other day trying to steal my wallet.

Halfway through the terrifying ordeal, I couldn't help but think to myself, "He's giving me a good run for my money."

You know what they say:

"Once you go black, you're a single mother."

I recently used the word "nigger" in front of my wife.

She said, "You can't say that, it's insulting. Say African-American instead."

Surely that's insulting them twice.

What does a black epileptic have written on his t-shirt?

"Help me, I'm not breakdancing!"

I just used my wife's shampoo 'for coloured hair'.

Now I've got a fucking Afro.

On the way home from work tonight, I suddenly blacked out.

I joined a gang, stabbed an old lady, raped her, lost my job, sold some drugs, pimped out my sister and then moaned about the white man for the rest of the night.

My wife and I were called in to see the headmaster at our daughter's school today because she's been making racist jibes at the black children.

We were absolutely horrified! We've always told her not to speak to them.

I walked by two black guys the other day and I heard one of them saying, "Black guys are way better than white guys."

Maybe I shouldn't have said, "Wait one cotton-picking minute..."

My house was burgled the other night. When the police arrived, they asked me, "Did you happen to see, or can you tell us anything about, the burglar?"

"Well... it was rather dark," I replied.

The police officer says, "Okay... and how tall was it?"

I don't think he understood me very well.

How do you stop a nigger raping your wife?

Seriously, he's been going at it for hours now and she should have had my fucking tea on the table twenty minutes ago!

What's the one word beginning with N and ending with R that you don't want to call a black person?

"Neighbour!"

During my driving lesson today, the instructor told me to pull over to the side and stop. When I did this, he told me to examine the road ahead.

"Okay, now point out what, in your mind, are the biggest hazards in the area ahead?" he asked.

"Well, those niggers on the corner look pretty shifty to me," I said.

Apparently that was wrong.

How do we know two wrongs don't make a right?

Black couples don't have white children!

Trading standards finally admitted why golliwogs were banned from marmalade labels.

It's because niggers were peeling them off and using them as bus passes!

In an equal opportunities seminar at work today, I was asked where I stood on racism.

Apparently "With the Whites" was not an appropriate response.

What has eight legs and a big black cunt?

The A-team.

I asked my black mate, "Do you prefer to be called black or coloured?"

He said, "Well, I'd prefer it if you called me Kevin."

I had a big heavy black woman bouncing on my cock last night. I remember thinking, I wish she was a bit lighter.

And didn't weigh as much.

I bumped into a black guy today.

"Go back to where you came from," I told him.

I'm really helpful in mazes.

Excuses for being late

I got here on time but, as I was walking through the gates, a wasp attacked me and chased me all the way back home again.

I have to go the doctor's because I have a hole in my bum.

I got stuck on the bus because a fat lady was blocking the exit.

I have short term memory loss and couldn't remember where I was going.

I was charged with rape again last night.

I'm sorry for being late for work, I was just collecting my unemployment benefits.

Sorry, we ran out of toilet paper.

It was foggy this morning and I accidentally walked into the wrong office and started working.

"My uncle died."

"Oh. Are you okay, mate? Were you close?"

"Yeah, he lived just round the corner."

Sorry boss, I was having a wank and my computer crashed. Took fucking ages to find where I was again.

I got the lift up to the ninth floor, but then realised I was scared of lifts so went back down to the ground floor and took the stairs instead.

Sorry I'm late, I slept in and the car wouldn't start. Wait a fucking minute - I'm self-employed!

It was foggy the night before and the wife left the window open, so when I woke up this morning, I couldn't find my socks.

I have a phobia of being late for work and I was trying to cure it by confronting it.

Sorry, I was up all night. And that kept me awake.

My daughter was violently mauled by next door's dog. You try walking any faster with an erection like this.

Sorry I'm late, I came on the bus and the driver made me clean it up.

I would have been here on time but there weren't any buses without Pakistanis with rucksacks for ages.

I'd rather be late than dead.

I was actually on time this morning, but I stood outside my office for half an hour trying to think of an excuse.

I slept with my window open. It was cold and my alarm clock froze.

I'm not coming into work today, I'm retired.

My psychiatrist says it is best to avoid situations where I am tempted to use a sub machine gun until the anti-psychotics have kicked in or the cunts have already died of natural causes.

Sorry I'm late. My neighbour was bathing his daughter and asked me to help.

Religion - Christianity

I just saw a book with the title 'Christianity for Dummies'

I don't understand why it wasn't just called 'Christianity'

I don't understand Christians.

They say that gambling is wrong, then bet their entire life on there being a heaven.

For Dads there is Father's Day,

For Mums there is Mother's Day,

For Lovers there is Valentine's Day,

And for Wankers there is Palm Sunday

Erm, so you're asking me to promise not to tell lies...

...by swearing upon the Bible?

A woman whose daughter was hospitalised in a US tornado told ITV News that "God would make her better."

Presumably, that's a different God from the one that almost killed her with a tornado.

How did Jesus feel about being crucified?

Cross.

Anyone else find it funny that the disclaimer "The characters in this film are fictitious and any resemblance to persons living or dead is purely coincidental" is in the credits for 'The Passion of the Christ'?

Today my girlfriend received a religious leaflet describing how abstinence is the only 100% effective way of avoiding pregnancy.

Outraged, I promptly sent the organisation a letter with a picture of Mary and Jesus and the caption "99.9%, you fucks."

I am not sure why all the Christian groups get so upset about same sex marriages. For years I have been in a same sex marriage.

I have been having the same sex in the same position with the same woman ever since I married the bitch - isn't that what they want?

I love Jesus.

He's born, I get presents. He dies, I get chocolate.

What did Jesus say to his twelve apostles as he was being nailed to the cross?

"Don't touch my fucking Easter eggs, I'll be back on Monday."

I saw a guy with a sticker that said 'Jesus is my co-pilot' on his car bumper.

When I overtook him, I noticed that Jesus was a small, fat lady with no teeth.

A teacher spotted little Johnny drawing pictures.

She asks, "What are you drawing?"

"I'm drawing God," little Johnny replies.

The teacher paused and then says, "But nobody knows what he looks like."

"They will in a minute," he replies.

They say that when you die you become closer to God.

Probably because you no longer fucking exist.

Religion - Catholics

I really hate it when other people force their religion down your throat.

Catholic priests are especially known for doing this.

A Catholic boy lying is seriously injured after being hit by a car outside a church.

A man runs to him and says, "Would you like me to fetch a priest, my son?"

The boy replies, "Can't you see I'm fucking dying? Sex is the last thing on my mind."

What's the difference between acne and a Catholic priest?

Acne doesn't come on a boy's face until he's thirteen or so.

What does a Catholic priest have in common with a pint of Guinness?

If you get a bad one, they both have serious repercussions for your arse.

I see the Catholic Church is finally moving with the times by allowing condoms to be used.

I suppose forensics are getting pretty advanced these days.

The Catholic Church has launched a hotline for victims of sex abuse.

Nice try, Church, but one already exists. It's called "The Police".

The Pope has stated that homosexual activity threatens the future of the human race.

I would have thought that all the kids put off sex for life by the most efficient paedophile organisation in the world disguised as a religion would have had a much more devastating effect.

I really don't get why we needed the Pope to visit the UK. I mean, what does he do?

He's like a school hamster that gets replaced with the same name when the old one dies so the children won't cry.

After 24 hours on Twitter, the Pope has a shitload of followers and hasn't even said anything yet...

Just like God.

BBC NEWS - The Pope calls for action on sex abuse.

Right after he called, "Lights...Camera..."

What do you call a nun in a wheelchair?

Virgin mobile.

What's the definition of innocence?

A nun working in a condom factory, thinking she's making sleeping bags for mice.

The new nun goes to her first confession and tells the priest that she has a terrible secret.

She says, "Father, I forgot to put any knickers on today and I am naked under my robe."

The priest says, "Bless you, my child. Say five Hail Marys, five Our Fathers, and do five cartwheels on your way to the altar."

Religion - Jewish

How do you tell if Jews are living next door to you?

There is wet toilet paper hanging on the clothesline.

A Jewish man takes his wife to hospital. She has two black eyes, no teeth and a broken nose.

The doctor says, "What happened?"

The Jew replies, "She was going through the change."

"What? The change? This doesn't happen in the change!"

"It does when it's in my fucking pocket!"

On a scale of Jordan to Jewish, how tight are you?

My boss is such a typical Jew.

If you come into work late, he docks your pay.

If you come into work early, he charges you rent.

Did you hear about the Jewish paedophile?

He comes out from behind the bushes and says, "Hey little boy, want to buy some sweets?"

As a man of Jewish descent, I don't like jokes about us Jews: I think they often cement prejudices and misinterpretations of the Jewish people and culture.

But, every now and then, even I enjoy a good laugh and feel that I shouldn't be so serious about everything.

So I have a very good joke about the Holocaust here, if anyone wants to buy it.

What's the difference between Harry Potter and the Jews?

Harry Potter made it out of the chamber.

Apparently, calling all the Jews that survived the Holocaust "Oven dodgers" is an easy way to get your history exam torn up.

Why do Jewish fathers have their sons circumcised?

They know Jewish women can't resist anything with 10% off.

Hitler may have killed six million Jews, but he sure as fucking hell saved the History Channel.

I raped a Jewish girl the other day. It was amazing, she was so fucking tight!

She used my phone to call the police afterwards.

Religion - Muslim

Just been to my first Muslim birthday party.

The musical chairs was a bit slow but, fuck me, the pass the parcel was quick!

I hear stories about a new kind of toilet paper being sold.

There's a drawing of the prophet Mohammed on it and you get to colour him in!

My new Muslim Girlfriend keeps talking about a blowjob.

I don't know whether to get my cock out or to warn London transport.

What's Islam and a sat-nav got in common?

You think you're on the right path but, follow them literally, and you'll end up smashing into a fucking building.

Some people are so ignorant and narrow minded. Not all Muslims are terrorists you know.

Some are taxi drivers.

What do you get after you win a religious debate against a Muslim?

Death threats.

Say what you like about Muslim women, they make brilliant bee keepers.

My wife told me about a Muslim woman who was lingering around the ladies showers at the pool, refusing to undress or remove her veil.

"She was just staring at the other women through her veil making everyone feel really uncomfortable. I think we should ban the burka."

"Now hold on honey, we shouldn't force people to adapt to our culture because of our own insecurities."

Besides, I love my burka disguise.

We asked 100 Muslim women about the burka, and they all claimed that they love wearing it.

Mind you, they all look the same. For all we know, we interviewed the same deluded bitch a hundred times.

I saw a nun walking over a frozen pond yesterday. Then, to my horror, she fell through the ice. I ran over to help and, as she put out her hand for me to grab, I realised it wasn't a nun, it was a Muslim woman in a burka.

I wonder if she managed to get herself out.

There's a Muslim bloke at work who eats pork, smokes, drinks alcohol, never prays and is constantly cheating on his wife.

He's a Shi'ite Muslim.

I was in the crazy maze at Alton Towers the other day. I turned a corner and there were four Muslim women in burkas. I shouted "Allah is a Cunt!" and ran for it.

Best game of Pac-Man I ever had!

If you burn a Koran, a Muslim may burn your house down.

The joke's on him: my house is full of Korans.

Religion - Other Religions

I bet Jehovah's Witnesses have some good knock-knock jokes...

A Jehovah's Witness knocked on my door and asked if I'd like to let Jesus into my home.

"Jesus can come in," I said, "but you can fuck off."

A Jehovah's Witness knocked on my door last night and my wife made me go to the door.

The Jehovah's Witness said, "Have you got some spare time to talk?"

I said, "Unfortunately not, I'm off to the pub, but my wife has. Come on in, she's behind the couch."

My favourite part about Halloween is seeing all the confused Jehovah's Witnesses wandering around, wondering why they've been given sweets.

Scientology - Taking the heat off of Jehovah's Witnesses since 1952.

My wife left me for a Hindu man. At least he'll treat her better.

They worship cows.

I can't take Scientology seriously. It's the belief that humans were brought to earth by aliens on a spaceship carried by two massive lizards, which landed in a volcano and dispersed humans throughout the world. Then the aliens take off, and the lizards go and hide under the sea in massive caves.

Add two Italian plumbers to that and you've got the first five levels of Super Mario!

When I was younger, I thought Mormons were lucky because of that multiple wife thing. I thought it must be great to have as many sexy wives as they wanted.

Then I got married and now I just feel sorry for the cunts.

MGMT isn't actually an acronym, it's the word 'management' condensed to four letters.

It took me a while to discover that BDSM has surprisingly little to do with Buddhism.

I don't get Creationists.

They can't grasp the concept of an ape-like creature evolving into a man, yet they have no problem with a rib turning into a woman.

Good news. Bad News

The good news is that I came back from South Africa with a lovely suntan. The bad news is I've got skin cancer.

The good news is you're pregnant, the bad news is it's a ginger.

The bad news is we had to amputate both your legs. The good news is the bloke in the next bed wants to buy your slippers.

The bad news is your kids got cancer. The good news is DISNEYLAND! And not the shitty French one either.

The good news is on BBC. The bad news is on Sky.

The good news is our syndicate won £6.4 million on the lottery. The bad news is I forgot to put the numbers on.

The good news is our syndicate won £6.4 million on the lottery. The bad news is there's 6.4 million of us in the syndicate.

The good news is your dad has built an underground extention! The bad news is your going to have to spend most of your childhood there.

The good news is she adores me, especially my youthful looks. The bad news is I'm in jail for another forty years.

The bad news is that I'm dyslexic. The gud neiwo fclwdkfvoij iz alkdm enofs vik.

The good news is you'll only ever hear one more bit of bad news. The bad news? ....**BANG!!!**

Sex and Shit - Masturbation & Porn

I recently suggested to my wife that she try masturbating with fruit.

She went fucking bananas.

My six-year-old son caught me masturbating this morning.

He said, "What are you doing daddy?"

"It's called wanking," I replied. "You'll be doing this soon."

"Why, daddy?" he asked.

"Because my arm is fucking killing me."

They say the best thing about internet porn is there are no pages to get stuck together.

True, but I daren't close my laptop for fear I'd never get it open again.

Man: "How much for a wank?"

Prostitute: "£15"

Man: "Thanks. I don't want one, I just wanted to know how much I was saving every night."

We were sat on the sofa tonight and my wife held my hand.

I glanced down and said, "Do you fancy an early night?"

She winked, "Go on then."

"I was talking to my hand," I replied.

My dad sat me down, brought the laptop in and said, "Son, I think it's time to talk to you about pornography."

"What about it?" I asked.

"How the hell can I get past the filters without your mum knowing?"

I clicked on a link saying 'Bald and Barely Legal' yesterday.

Unzipping and firming up, I waited for the page to load.

It was a Department of Transport website about car tyres.

I cannot stand watching porn.

I find I wank better sitting down.

I was on the laptop earlier and the wife said, "You're always on that bloody thing. What would you be doing if the internet hadn't been invented?"

I said, "Probably still wanking over that photo of your sister."

According to scientists, watching porn makes men see women just as sex objects. Well, I think that's totally untrue. I watch porn and don't just see my wife as a sex object.

She's also a cook, a cleaner and something to hit when I'm bored.

The Judge studied each picture in sequence before looking up at me.

"Without doubt, these are the sickest, most perverted images I have even been confronted with. It almost beggars belief that, inebriated or not, young women would allow such photographs to be taken....."

He paused before opening his wallet. "Fifty quid for the lot, you said?"

You know you masturbate too much when you drop your wank sock and your wife shouts from the other room, "I hope that wasn't one of our good plates."

I see our local men's clothes shop is doing a special for singles.

Buy two socks, get another one free.

I got talking to a woman at the bus stop yesterday and she mentioned her seven-year-old daughter had been asking awkward sex questions.

"Tell me about it," I said.

"Oh, are you in the same boat?" she asked.

"No," I said, "I just really fancy a wank."

Sex and Shit - Incest

One in four girls in America has a problem with incest. Just goes to show how fucked up their country really is...

Three out of four girls don't mind it.

I was working late at the Carphone Warehouse last night when I received this text from my daughter, "Dad,thespacebuttonisfaultyonthisphone.

Whenyougethomepleasegivemeanalternative."

And as I eagerly rushed home, I couldn't help but wonder...

What the hell does 'ternative' mean?

It's so awkward when you send a private text message to the wrong person.

The other day I wrote a message, "Hey babe, thinking of U makes my cock hard, can't wait to sex U up 2night" and sent it to my ten-year-old daughter.

Imagine how embarrassing it would have been if I'd sent that to the wrong person.

I overheard my daughter and her pals saying they were going to the club tonight to enter a wet T-shirt competition.

I'll be the judge of that.

The cops have just charged me with fucking arson.

They should see what I've done with our daughter.

I came home from work early today and caught my daughter masturbating with a cucumber.

"That's disgusting," I said. "I'm meant to be eating that tonight, now it's going to taste like salad."

My wife just said, "It's your turn next, what do you want for Father's Day?"

"A blowjob" I replied.

"Ha-ha, but what do you want from your daughter?"

I am sick to death of repeating myself to that woman.

I remember when I was eight-years-old and my dad gave me a warning about anal sex.

He said, "This is going to hurt a bit."

Being wanked off and cooking are pretty similar.

Plenty of people will do it for you, but your Nan does it best.

When my daughter's first serious boyfriend came round to pick her up for a date, I thought I'd better do the fatherly thing and take him to one side for a little chat about sex.

"Now then, David", I said to him, "Before you take my daughter out, I just want to know whether you've got any condoms?"

"Yes, sir, as a matter of fact I do," he answered, squirming with embarrassment.

"Well son, if you do manage to get Claire into bed then you needn't bother with them, I've had her on the pill since she was twelve," I replied. "Oh and, David, make sure you bite her nipples and slap her about a bit," I added. "She likes it rough".

Sex and Shit - Gay

My gay brother has recently been diagnosed with HIV

What a bummer.

Just after my wife had given birth, I asked the doctor, "How soon do you think we'll be able to have sex?"

He winked at me and said, "I'm off duty in ten minutes. Meet me in the car park."

My doctor was checking my balls for any lumps the other day.

It got awkward when I ran my fingers through his hair.

I just walked into my son's bedroom to find him performing a horrific homosexual act.

He was sat there reading Twilight.

I said to my mate, "If you keep smoking like that, you'll be dead soon".

He said, "Smoking like what?"

I said, "The way you're holding it: you look like a queer. This is a rough area."

The wife and I had been thinking that it was about time that we told our teenage son that he was adopted. We sat him down and I said, "Son, there is something that your mother and I want to say and I want you to know this is the hardest thing we've ever had to do."

He said, "I know what you're going to say... It's true, I'm gay."

I said, "Well, thanks for making what I'm about to do a fucking pleasure."

A little boy knocked on my door and said, "Is Jimmy coming out?"

I said, "I doubt it mate, he's only five. He hasn't even tried women yet."

My son came up to me with tears in his eye and said, "Dad, I'm gay. Can you still love me?"

"Don't be silly, son," I replied. "You were an accident, we never loved you."

My gay son came downstairs today and said, "Dad, have you seen the straighteners?"

"Yeah, right here, son," I replied, massaging my knuckles.

I've been gasping for a fag all day.

Which is one of the problems of being an asthmatic homosexual.

Mother: "I think our son's gay."

Father: "What makes you think that?"

Mother: "Have you seen the skid marks in his undies?"

Father: "Yeah, but even we have skiddies in ours now and then."

Mother: "True - but not at the fucking front."

Nine out of ten men prefer large boobs.

The other man prefers the nine men.

"So," I asked, "Are you still on for a cock up your arse later?"

My wife looked shocked, "I can't believe you just asked me that in front of the whole pub!"

"Really?" I replied. "I can't believe you thought I was talking to you. Come on, Ron, let's get out of here."

Sex and Shit - Oral Sex

There was a survey on why men liked blowjobs.

5% liked the look, 15% liked the feel and the other 80% liked the silence!

On the eve of our anniversary, my wife and I agreed that whoever woke up first in the morning should wake the other one with oral sex.

Come the morning, I was up first so I slowly pulled back the covers...

... and stuck my cock in her mouth.

A warning to all men: women are using date rape drugs called blowjobs to lure men into scams called relationships.

My wife said that my penis closely resembles a Tic Tac.

She was proud of her remark, until I asked her why her sister still had bad breath.

My mate looked at me and said, "Would you suck a Paki's dick for a million pounds?"

I replied, "Put your dick away, Abdul, you haven't got a million pounds."

I came home from the pub early to catch my son getting a blowjob from his girlfriend.

I said, "Just you wait until your mother gets home."

He said, "Why do we have to tell her?"

I said, "So your girlfriend can give her some tips."

I was suddenly awoken with a blow job this morning.

That's the last time I fall asleep on the train with my mouth open.

My girlfriend only gives me a blowjob if I wear a condom.

That's like taking a shit with your boxers on.

I've just found a robot that's made purely for blow jobs.

I'm not going to buy one though, it was obviously made by a gay man.

Why else would it be called "Henry"?

I'm sick of people knocking on my door, begging.

There's just been a woman asking for donations for a sperm bank.

I gave her a right fucking mouthful.

When my wife came home last Sunday afternoon to find the kitchen and living room a mess, the laundry still in a pile by the washer and me asleep on the couch having done nothing but drink beer and watch telly all day, she yelled, "Watch yourself, Mister, or you're going to make me do something I don't want to do."

I thought, "I can't believe it... I'm going to get a fucking blow job out of this!"

I stopped my car beside a prostitute last night.

As she got in I asked, "How much for a blow job?"

She said, "Thirty quid."

I said, "Can you do twenty?"

"Yeah, okay," she replied.

I said, "Great, here's £600 then."

Sex and Shit - Anal Sex

A recent survey has shown that 50% of all newlyweds want to try anal sex.

Or, to put it another way, 100% of grooms.

I was fucking my secretary up the arse when my wife walked in.

She said, "You can't do this to me!"

I said, "I know... that's why I'm doing it to her."

Anal sex: It's not for pussies.

My girlfriend was putting sun cream on.

"Do you mind doing my back?" she asked.

"Let's pretend I'm your butler," I winked. "My name's Dawes."

"Okay!" she giggled, "Would you mind doing my back, Dawes?"

And that was all the invitation I needed.

Having a girl with a tattoo on the back of her neck is much like having a bathroom with a magazine in it.

It gives you something to read while you're in the shitter.

Tried anal for the first time last night.

I don't think I'm going to like prison.

I was driving down a dark country lane when I shunted the car in front at a junction.

The lady got out and yelled, "I don't believe this... fancy ramming me up the arse!"

And that, your honour, is where the misunderstanding started...

I took a girl back to my place last night.

As I was fucking her on my bed, I pulled out a huge bottle of lube and said, "Do you mind if I put it up your arse?"

She looked at me and said, "Is it going to hurt?"

I said, "Probably, it's a big bottle."

I don't usually mind my doctor being so tongue-in-cheek.

Just not when I'm having my prostate examined.

Had a bit of back door action with the wife when I got back from the pub last night.

She locked me out so I had to kick it in.

My girlfriend's dad really hates me, and when I was last over at her house, he kept getting me to do favours for him.

"Go get us a beer would you, son? Oh and, while you're at it, could you make me a sandwich?"

When I returned, he had a smug grin on his face and sarcastically said, "I'm not being a pain in the arse, am I?"

"Don't worry about it," I replied. "I'm often a pain in your daughter's arse."

Sex and Shit - Sex

A wise man once said to me, "Women are like toilets. They're all dirty apart from the disabled ones."

I beg to differ. Last night I was shagging a disabled girl and she pissed all over me without me even asking.

If you have sex with a prostitute without her permission, is it rape or shoplifting?

My wife asked me how I could love her and still enjoy watching porn.

I told her, I love my car, but I still watch Formula 1 too.

She was happy with this analogy.

I just never mentioned I also go to Hertz for the occasional rental.

Note to self: when hiring a prostitute whilst on holiday in Amsterdam, never again ask her to "sit on my face" in a 'shilly Dutch akshent'.

I'm always frank with my sexual partners.

Don't want them knowing my real name, do I?

I had to defrost the fridge last night before bed.

Or foreplay, as she calls it.

If you can legally have sex when you're sixteen, but you can't watch porn until you're eighteen, shouldn't sixteen-to-seventeen-year-olds be having sex blindfolded?

I was busy having sex with the wife when I felt a tap on my shoulder.

I hate fucking in the bath.

I stayed at my girlfriend's dad's house last night.

We raided his cupboards for alcohol and ended up getting very drunk and having sex in his bed.

My girlfriend thinks I stayed at my gran's.

A young lady went to the doctor for a physical.

Afterwards, the doctor said, "You're in perfect health, except for those abrasions on your knees."

The woman replied, "Oh, those are carpet burns from having sex doggie-style."

The doctor asked, "Don't you know any other positions?"

She answered, "Yeah, but my dog doesn't!"

My wife and I were enjoying a little bedtime action last night.

Just at the point of orgasm, there was a scream of, "Oh, Oh yes, Oh, Oh Johnny Depp!"

We stopped.

"You think of other men when we're having sex?"

"Well, sometimes, but don't feel bad about it. It doesn't mean anything," I said.

I went into a brothel and said, "How much for anal?"

She said, "Sixty quid."

I said, "Ah, that's a bit expensive. I think I'll leave it."

She said, "Tight arse."

I said, "Oh, go on then."

What's the best part about having sex with twenty eight year olds?

There's twenty of them!

Sex and Shit - The Wife

I was shagging the wife last night and, after coming for the second time, I rolled over.

My wife was not impressed and said, "How about finishing me off now?"

So I smothered her with my pillow.

My wife had a job interview for a camera store the other day.

Before she left, she knew I'd have a joke lined up, and so she said, 'Please don't give me any of your silly puns like "you're a snappy dresser" or "it'll be over in a flash."'

So I punched her in the face, and said, "That bruise should develop in about an hour and if you interrupt my jokes again, well, you get the picture..."

A woman's fanny is like a shed roof.

If you don't nail it hard enough, it will end up next door.

I think my girlfriend has had sixty-one boyfriends before me.

She calls me her sixty-second lover.

My wife's fanny smells like roses.

But Rose's fanny is tighter.

I was in the pub with my girlfriend last night when she said, "Can I ask you a question?"

"Sure, babe," I replied, stroking her hair. "What is it?"

She said, "Why are you with me?"

I said, "Because I love you."

She said, "I know, but this is the ladies toilets and I'm trying to have a shit."

My girlfriend's pretty thick - everything goes over her head.

Fortunately, so do both her feet, so we're still good.

A charity worker knocked on my door this morning and said, "Hi, sir, we are in the area collecting for victims of domestic abuse."

I said, "Hold on a minute, I'll shout for my wife. TINA, SOMEBODY AT THE DOOR WITH SOME MONEY FOR YOU."

My wife went mental when she found a sex tape of me with a young, fit brunette in the wardrobe.

Her mood didn't really improve when I pointed out the tape was of her from ten years ago, before she had kids and let herself go.

My wife complained that I'm always trying to be someone I'm not.

I'm wondering how the fuck she got into the Batcave.

Me and the wife have been playing "Call of Duty" tonight.

I've been phoning her up to check she's doing the washing, cooking and cleaning.

My wife said, "I want a divorce and half of everything you have."

So I put 50,000 indecent images of children on her laptop and called the police.

When I got divorced, my wife said she would fight for custody of the kids.

Took her out with one fucking punch.

Sex and Shit - Blondes

I raped a blonde woman last night.

As I finished and casually walked off, she shouted, "I'll get you back for this."

I just laughed, but the next evening I was walking through the same spot when she suddenly jumped out of the bushes onto my back and pulled me to the ground.

She ripped my jeans off, sat on my cock and said, "How do you like it, you bastard?"

I went on a date with a blonde last night.

"Do you have any kids?" she asked.

"Yes," I replied, "I have one child that's under two."

She said, "I might be blonde, but I know how many one is."

I was shagging my blonde girlfriend when she said, "Come all over me and I will not leave your bedroom until I've licked it all up."

Three years on, she's still in my bedroom. Fuck knows how my jizz got onto her elbow.

I was on the phone to my blonde wife. "I'm near home love, put the kettle on."

After a ten-second pause, I said, "Hello, you still there?"

"Yeah," she replied. "I don't think the kettle wants to talk right now."

A blonde just texted me saying, "What does IDK stand for?"

I texted back saying, "I don't know" and she replied, "OMG, no-one does!"

As I knelt down with a pair of size 4 shoes in front of this sexy blonde in a short skirt, I couldn't resist a quick glance at her knickers.

"Hey, cheeky!" she said as she gave me a playful kick. "I bet the only reason you work here is to look up girls' skirts, isn't it?"

"That's an absolutely ridiculous accusation, madam," I said sternly. "I don't fucking work here!"

I ran into the vet's this morning and said to the blonde receptionist, "Quick, I think my daughter's hamster is in serious trouble."

"Hamster?" she laughed. "That's a snake."

A blonde was admitted into hospital for having phone sex.

Doctors removed two Nokias, one Samsung and two Motorolas, but no Siemens were found.

My wife rang me "Quick, come home!" she shouted in a panicked voice. "Some young girl has broken into our house and has tied herself up in the cellar."

That's why I married a blonde.

They say you can't beat a pretty blonde with big tits.

Nonsense. I have a restraining order for doing precisely that.

I was sat in a cafe earlier when a blonde looked up to catch me watching her eat her banana.

She started sucking on it, gave me a wink and said, "Teasing you, am I?"

"You sure are," I replied. "I could murder a banana right now."

My blonde wife burnt my salad today.

How fucking stupid can somebody be?

I told her that, from now on, I'll be cooking my own salad.

The Rules!

If you can grow a beard, you should not be on a skateboard.

You shouldn't wear skinny jeans if you can't fill them.

Having said which, filling your jeans is frowned upon.

When it's your round, get up and get the fuckin' beer in!

Always leave one urinal between you and anyone else in the toilet.

Don't wash your arse with the face cloth.

Don't play with fire, or other potentially dangerous things.

Real men do not punch holes in thin plasterboard walls.

Never ask a pensioner how they are.

If your friend is chatting up a girl, leave him the fuck alone.

Don't do your friend's sister unless she's really hot.

If your friend is chatting up your hot sister, knock him the fuck out.

When you have got back in your car after filling up at a petrol station, try to remember you are not the pilot of an aircraft and your car does not need a 17 point safety check before you pull away. Just start your engine and fuck off!

DON'T FUCKING WEAR FUCKING SUNGLASSES FUCKING IN-FUCKING-DOORS.

Always look over your shoulder before telling a racist joke.

If someone tells you a secret that you must never tell anyone ever, it means you can only tell one person at a time.

Friendzone is not conclusive, a prison sentence is.

Other - Football

Ever noticed that during international football matches, the score shows three letters to indicate which country is playing which, such as 'ENG 3-0 FRA'?

I wonder if that's why I've never seen NIGeria play GERmany

Dear Sickipedia,

I have 23 jokes and I can't understand why any of them haven't scored very well.

Fabio.

Three Celtic fans walk into a bar... A priest, a poof and a paedophile.

And that was just the first one.

Tough game for Liverpool tomorrow.

Football.

To all those women who watch the football and shout "Pass it to Frank!" or "Bring Joe Cole on!": fuck off. You didn't see me at Sex And The City 2 shouting "Fuck her up the arse!"

England v USA - Kick off 19:30.

USA will turn up at 19:41 and then claim victory.

So the Germans have said that England's "goal" being disallowed is fine and acceptable as it was simply karma for the Russian Linesman Incident in '66.

Well said Germany; and, on a similar note, I have opened a wonderfully legitimate new recreational shower chamber that six million of you should pop along to, free of charge, and discuss the ins and outs of your karma theory.

I met a fairy today who granted me one wish. "I want to live forever," I said.

"Sorry," said the fairy, "I'm not allowed to grant wishes like that."

"Fine," I said. "I want to die when West Brom win the Premier League."

"You crafty cunt!" said the fairy.

Two policemen were horrified to find a number of the Northern Ireland football team playing football with a hedgehog yesterday.

They were just about to phone the RSPCA when they realised that the hedgehog was beating them four-nil.

You really do have to feel sorry for all those Villa fans travelling home.

Aston is a fucking shit hole.

Be on the lookout for a new breed of 'Evil- Manc' computer viruses that could seriously affect/infect your PC.

There are many varieties of this virus, each affecting your computer in a different way. Details of each variant of this virus are shown below.

The Manchester United virus - This where the computer develops a memory disorder and forgets about everything before 1993.

The Manchester United Shirt virus - Designed to drain your bank account. This one is especially hard to detect as it changes its format every three months.

The David Beckham virus - This affects newer computers mainly. The computer looks great, all the lights are on, but nothing works.

The Roy Keane virus - Throws you out of Windows.

The Alex Ferguson virus - The computer develops a continuous whining noise. The on screen clock runs a lot slower than all the other computers in the building.

The Solskjaer virus - Will take numerous attempts to get into the net, often failing completely.

The Ryan Giggs virus - The computer develops a processor problem, whereby it thinks it's better than it actually is. It also experiences dramatic fluctuations in performance.

The Fabien Barthez virus - You just can't save anything.

The Laurent Blanc virus - Makes your computer go really slowly and creates big holes in your hard-drive.

The Phil Neville virus - The worst of all: ruins all memory of basic functions and programmes, randomly delivering data to the wrong goal. Also weakens all communications within the network.

The Dressing Room virus - Appears when the system fails. Reboot may be dangerous.

Football: The legal way to buy a nigger.

A pound coin was thrown onto the pitch at Ibrox.

Police are trying to determine whether it was a missile or a takeover bid.

Blackpool are 500/1 to win the Premier League next year.

Which means if you put just £20 on them at the start of the season, you will lose £20.

I went out and bought FIFA the other day.

It's great being the president of Qatar.

The police rescued a small lad from his parents who beat him constantly. He was placed with an aunt, who sadly beat him too. Then he went to a foster home, where again he was beaten.

He has now been placed with the England football team who, as we know, cannot beat anyone.

What's the difference between Newcastle United and the Bermuda Triangle?

The Bermuda Triangle has three points.

I'm looking forward to the African Nations Cup.

My money's on Chelsea.

When Brendan Rodgers said he thought Liverpool could finish second, I didn't realise he meant in every game.

It's a year ago today since my Dad passed.

Greedy bastard just tries to shoot every time he gets the ball now.

BBC News: England Women not expected to win the World Cup.

Oh well, back to the chopping board.

Liverpool: "Hi lads, how much for Carroll?"

Newcastle: "35 million, lol j..."

Liverpool: "Done."

Teacher to class: **"What does your dad do at weekends?"**

Little Boy: **"He's a dancer in a gay bar and sometimes, if the money's right, he lets punters bang his arse and cum in his gob."**

Teacher takes him outside: **"Is that true?"**

Little boy: "No, miss, its bollocks. He plays for Derby County, but I'm too embarrassed to say."

Mark Lawrenson, during the Germany v Italy game: "Germany need to step on the gas."

Woah Mark... let's not encourage them to do that again!

Why do so many housewives love Arsenal?

Because they stay on top for ages and then come second.

The kids from Alder Hey hospital are going to Anfield today to cheer the players up.

I came home from work and my wife said, "I washed your England shirt for you today."

I said, "What England shirt?"

She said, "The red one that was in the frame on the wall. Whoever Bobby Moore is, tell him to stop drawing all over your clothes."

Wayne Rooney - "United have won so many trophies I can't count."

He's missing a full stop after trophies there.

Knorr have released a special edition black and white striped Oxo cube to celebrate the Newcastle United's Premier League season.

It's called the Laughing Stock.

The FA have announced a three-way joint shirt sponsorship deal with an oil company, a designer clothing brand and a parcel delivery firm.

The shirt sponsor logos will read:

Total

fcuk

UPS

After years of seeking him, America finally offered $100,000,000 for Bin Laden.

Man City subsequently offered $105,000,000

Well done England, you've managed to beat a country where the currency is cabbage.

Can somebody please notify Liverpool that, along with their lack of imagination, the correct grammar is 'A field', not 'An field'? Thanks.

I've just signed a sixty grand a week contract to play for Chelsea next season.

Just need to get them to sign it now.

Why is it that, every time Japan made a substitution, the same player was going back on?

I was playing Football Manager on my PC when I was offered the Scotland job.

I knew it was a shit squad with no future, so I declined the offer.

I then put the phone down and got back to Football Manager.

Women's football would be a lot more popular if they renamed it "22 girls 1 cup."

When Thierry Henry was signed to play at Arsenal again, they said, "You'll feel right at home here, everything's just as you left it."

Including the trophy cabinet.

I was at Spurs last week. The bloke next to me called me a cunt.

I was going to punch his lights out. But I couldn't be bothered walking around the pitch.

The RSPCA have acted very quickly after recent incidents at the Emirates Stadium.

If you see an Arsenal fan with a dog, please ask them to call 0800 4-2 4-3 4-4 for free advice on how to hold onto a lead.

I think Ji Sung Park is a very naturally talented football player.

He can play while he is still asleep.

It's predicted that, by 2025, you'll be no more than six feet away from an ex-Chelsea manager.

Barack Obama has announced that US defence spending will be cut to $660 billion a year, meaning that the USA no longer has the highest annual defence budget in the world.

That honour now goes to Manchester City.

I've applied for the England manager's job.

I know I won't get it, but it keeps the dole people off my back for another couple of weeks.

My mate made the mistake of applying for the Wolves job.

He's got to go for an interview on Monday.

Portsmouth: The only club where they encourage you to throw coins at the players.

I'm so excited.

Only three more Chelsea managers till Christmas!

I hope our bid for the 2018 World Cup is successful.

I've always wondered what it would be like to have people coming over here from all over the world.

What do you call a black man with no life goals?

Emile Heskey.

Wayne Rooney's gone to Dubai for his birthday.

He must have been saving up for that all day.

Seeing Man Utd on Channel 5 is a bit like seeing my daughter in a porno.

I'm disappointed but I'll still watch it.

I couldn't resist having a quick wank yesterday.

The ref booked me for an "over-elaborate" goal celebration.

My dog does a somersault every time Man United score a goal.

Sometimes he does two somersaults, it depends how hard I kick him.

The England football team are going to change the emblem on their shirts.

The Three Lions will now become three tampons, to celebrate their worst fucking period in history.

Me and my girlfriend have been together for a long time, and our favourite sexual position is the Scottish World Cup Squad.

Neither of us know what we're doing or why we're there, there's no passion, no communication and we never even make it past the first stage. It's often accompanied by a very bad soundtrack, horrible dribbling and never, ever a clean sheet. It's always over far too quickly and, when it does end, I know it will be at least another 12 years before it happens again.

There's a rumour going around that the police have said you're not allowed to wear England shirts in pubs in case it upsets Muslims.

What the fuck is a Muslim doing in a pub?

At least, after the 2022 World Cup, Qatar will have some cracking stadiums to stone women in.

When Saddam Hussein was found guilty he was originally sentenced to be shot.

His last request was to name his own firing squad: He chose Lampard, Gerrard and Carragher from 12 yards.

Other - Wordplay

A couple of naked lesbians barged into the house today, and started wrestling with my wife while she was in the bath.

I tried to help, but I could only knock one out.

Just been on bigbustycoons.com

Damn, those guys have really good bus companies.

When my girlfriend said she was leaving because of my obsession with The Monkees, I thought she was joking.

And then I saw her face.

My son is starting school soon and thinks the other children will pick on him because of his name.

I said, "Don't be silly, Someoneyourownsize, why would anyone pick on you?"

"Jesus loves you."

A nice gesture in church.

A horrific thing to hear in a Mexican prison.

I was talking to my wife today after our son got sent home early from school for swearing.

I said, "Apparently, he said the 'c' word."

She said, "Well that wasn't clever, was it?"

I replied, "No, it was 'cunt'."

One of the toddlers on the Intensive Care Unit is playing with a toy donkey.

ICU baby, shaking that ass.

I suggested to my wife that she'd look sexier with her hair back.

Which is apparently an insensitive thing to say to a cancer patient.

If you're always organizing things, you have OCD.

If you're always eating things, you have OBCD.

The kitchen staff really helps my wife get the cooking done quicker.

I say staff...really it's just a big stick I use to beat her.

This girl came up to me today and said she recognised me from Vegetarian Club.

I was confused, I'd never met herbivore.

I don't know why people have sex with women whilst they are on their period. Its bloody nuts if you ask me.

My daughter was running a temperature so I rang the doctor. He asked if she was hot.

I said, "Well, with a little make-up..."

My house was repossessed at the weekend but I don't blame the building society.

It's that fucking priest not doing the exorcism properly in the first place.

I spent some time at my wife's grave earlier.

She's not dead - she thinks I'm digging a pond.

Today I walked into a restaurant.

"Hi, is my table ready?"

"No, not yet sir. Do you mind waiting?"

"No, that's okay."

"Great, take these to table six then."

When a Jamaican talks to me about 'Shootings', I'm not sure whether they're talking about gunfire or footwear accessories.

Other - One-Liners

I was recently the subject of a joke. I chickened out of a fight and crossed the road to get away.

I'll stop at nothing to avoid using negative numbers.

I believe a lot of conflict in the Wild West could have been avoided completely if cowboy architects had just made their towns big enough for everyone.

Statistically, nein out of ten Germans are attractive.

Urinals. They take no shit.

I don't like being called a racist. I prefer ethnic critic.

Stable relationships are for horses.

Try braking: it gives your driving a bit of 00mph.

Trying to fart when you've got the shits is very similar to trying to sneeze when you're eating Coco Pops.

I got so excited in French lessons that sometimes "oui" would come out.

Sometimes I have sex with my wife before a long, passionate smoke.

It's all fun and games until you realise Casper the Ghost is actually a dead child.

Other - Misunderstandings

This guy from over the road was talking to me earlier.

"My wife's just told me she's been having an affair with Dave the milkman," he confided.

"What? That fat ugly fucker I see every morning outside your house?"

"Yes!" he laughed, cheering up.

"Why would Dave the milkman want to shag that?"

I've just received a text from my girlfriend that reads:

"Hello, birthday boy. When you get home from work, there'll be a hot bath waiting for you. When you've finished, come into the bedroom and I'll suck you dry ;)"

Fuck that, it'll take ages. I'll just use a towel.

I took a vase to get valued on the Antiques Roadshow and they told me it was 'absolutely priceless'.

Well, I got four quid for it at a car boot sale last weekend. Who's laughing now?

I was on the bus today when an inspector got on and said to me, "Ticket, please!"

Not one to make him feel embarrassed, I leant over and whispered, "You have to buy them off the driver, mate."

I was having a shit in the train toilet today when some bloke knocked on the door.

He said, "Can I see your ticket please?"

"Not right now," I shouted. "I'm having a shit!"

He said, "I don't believe you. Can you pass it under the door?"

"No problem," I said, sliding it under. "The yellow bits are sweetcorn."

I got a phone call last night to say that my wife had been in an accident.

I rushed to the hospital and asked the nurse, "How is she? Can I see her?"

She said, "I'm afraid you're too late."

I said, "Okay, no worries. I'll come back in the morning."

My mate said, "It's mine and the wife's tenth anniversary next weekend. I thought we could go somewhere really nice together."

"Sounds good to me, mate. What are you going to tell your wife though?"

I've been put on the waiting list for a new kidney.

It's a very exclusive butcher's.

There are many people who would love to have my girlfriend. She never says no to a shag, she's got great tits and even swallows.

But her bird collecting has gone far enough now.

"Doctor, my son's got a lump on his cock."

"How big is it?"

"Around four inches when erect. But I'm here about the lump."

"I'm sorry love, but do you take it up the arse? Or can you just swallow it?" I asked this fit bird down the drug store.

"Can you fuck off, you creep?!" she yelled back, "I'm sick of men like you thinking we're so easy."

"Listen, miss, can you calm the fuck down and tell me how I'm supposed to take these suppositories you've just sold me?" I replied.

Someone stole my newspaper this morning, so I quickly sneaked next door and took my neighbours.

Now that I've calmed down, I think kidnap may have been excessive.

The wife stormed indoors. "You bastard, I'll never get rid of that smell."

"But you said I could do it!" I replied.

"Like fuck I did!" she said.

"You did. I told you the toilet was blocked and I was desperate."

"But I told you to go to your mum's round the corner?" she stammered.

"Yes, and I didn't think I'd make it and you said, 'Here's my keys - go in my car!'"

"You have to tell me the truth," my barrister said. "It doesn't matter to me if you're guilty or not, I just don't want to be surprised in court."

"Okay, I raped and murdered those prostitutes," I admitted.

"Interesting, but can we get back to this shoplifting charge, please?"

Sickipedia Limericks

Sickipedia: the place for a joke
It is read by peculiar folk
Some good and some bad
Some definitely mad
And a couple that I'd like to poke!

A girl who grew up in a slum,
Was quite sad as she didn't have a mum
But what made her more sad
Was she DID have a dad
That stuck things he made up her bum

There once was a man from Devon
Whose daughter had just turned eleven
I took a look at her tush
Fucked her in a bush
And it turned out she was actually seven

I once had a ride on a cow
But I won't go near the things now
Though they have a big cunt
I do miss the grunt
So I'm going back to my sow

On a dirty weekend with my bird
That is the time I first heard
Her let off a fart in bed
Right next to my head
And next to me there laid a big turd

Here lays the body of Mary Fox
Who gave 500 men the pox
They started to itch
So got revenge on the bitch
By kicking her square in the box.

Goldilocks and the three bears
Decided to all go upstairs
They had a quick roll
She'd one in each hole
And her face was covered in hairs

I once shagged a girl up the bum
But as I was going to come
There came a loud knock at the door
I pushed little sis to the floor
And spurted my load over mum

THANKS FOR READING!

Visit Sickipedia.org, where you can find over 300,000 more hilarious jokes, and if you're brave enough, submit your own!

If you liked the book, please leave us a review, or better yet, buy a copy for your gran!

For press enquiries, marriage proposals, book signings or if you just fancy a chat, email us:
management@sickipedia.org

Contributors

Sickfuck, cuntballs, sw3llh34d, Ciabi, Biscuit777, treefella22, sickinthehead14, ray piste, Norma Snob, sick puppy, bumblesquash, Dristarg, miafay123, Cryogenic, mutsnuts, stallion sd, Little Red Rooster, WTD, krishand, wonderbrawl, torakrubik, ruari, karnsy123, sickblob, bungholebuster, roofus, DirtyCuntPJ, ClitCommander, DiscoStu, albinobob123, MikeLit, Spoon, RossGreen88, deepnuts, CathalSherry, mariners, bawbag, barry89, rickyapearman, ncoreas, bleary, gazzytee, commandercool84, Denver, alexorozco, cvrock, swampy123, boroboy, pedroflaps, 8 ace, RedderMist, kdivers, mickle, pally76, Fyffes, kitkat456, ShittyPants, Boogaloo, Cabron Monoxide, Sex from Sideways, Dicko1981, jnwwfc1, scooby99, Fubar, illegalnature, dobby218, drof, zip, DoubleTee, pep, pt, TomAllen, sam23, RaxTT, We Are The Lemmon, mg1, amber dextrous, pigchaser, oorwullie, blandy81, JesusWasABastard, mancbatterer, JulesClairon, kakheadman, 123max, Dangerfield, adamscott, NTD, xxxxxx, harvinator, creeper963, Pokemon-man, Fuzbomb, Fists Of Fuhrer, Veng Neng Yam, aliaSligo, jibjab, AndrewPrice, newzero, Racialdiscriminationiswrong, Jimmythetwat, mangiballs, Cumquat, PizzaofDeath, urhtone, Cooperman, what-a-joke, BeJesus, birkender999, y2j, mmmmmmm, justincider, jay1975, Reject Dog, Nevil1950, stu71, MRMIdAS, davidb2k, lookingforinspiration, titchio, coathanger, causty, stevo21, Stu-Tang, fuckface, sacredcow, Baldlice, tartanspartan, MichaelTimothyAwesome, matt.hellens, TGS, buddy_millet, turdbreath, Debbie McGhee, tOmmy8, gazman8412, David7Villa, badtaste_123, BoabyDylan, Mercman, Habbaz804, Apathetic, raycyst, mediator, mathb, xian, Gash TL, lukebell, hello95, zobbertron, sickhammie, Ramalam, Balfour, EvilDan, irbaboon, the masked avenger, jam_theman, nobscratcher, NickD1, viperuk, jaypindaouse, peebles, slightlymoist, Lovelace, kensai1230, MrStuPidtwat, albertgordon, beez, Roll , izzlebeef, ilolprick, tibip20, Space Bandito, gudtimecharlie, pottyonetoo, charlie1105, URANUS HERTZ, smokey ,abudanta, Sparkes, anthony4, rickroll13, 8PintsOnYourDoorstep, Dooh ,Timmytour, charlesda9, fistheadx36, Cleveland, mike_dale14, Super-Dave, Brotherfucker, famous amos ,Turbo-Tampon, richdick ,TykeThat, Julian999 ,danny75078, purespasticated, geebee, 9 Star ,ChaosAerodemon, taziker ,pornstar, furiousg, sainteebrian, HarshHilarity ,def-con-one ,million, ctr12345, agoodshit, shesonfire, fox in the box, Miggle, Bizlop ,Faceman, DavidCollorn, bonkbonk, comandhaveagoifyouthinkyourhardenough, grotesk, Tinpotbob , deanothepenguin, OkiPaul ,Sick Cunt, schlong69, caliban, stash, owd humper, grant17, cuntmeistergeneral, davidoff7, supa9, jazzinuk, vespa, city hobgoblin, wamphyri, Craig.M, ComedownWilly, DL2H, spiritleader, analCake, avg, joe kerr 199, bumfluffbobRG, oli, Milo, mituation, Firefox, laugingcow, marley, jamesyjames411, nick78, cric, coblefartthefirst, drunkenoaf, Bazza2103, caffeine_free, Django, gregoire, fatuous_sunbeam, Fuckdat, electriclight, getdad777, NinjaFuzz, immortalshower666, Fludder, Rexton, DDJ, VYCENESS3, Greeno, BadHashMan, ht, Swoosher7797, Noddy-no-nose, davecrocket, Ihavepornontheothertab, sodomicity, jonowev, eviltorry, princessstreacle, JoeSeddon, bighelmet, ballscunt, TUNA45, Rocket11, soupy227, max the storyteller, Jake Blackwell, Tappity, Get Wild, inferno, jeizus, vagina transplanterss, docvoorhees, thew, Sacro, pissingonviKINGS, philsboro, Steedee, rwpunk, gangrath, shortly, tdfboy, Kristow, MilesOffTheMark, SuSu, CookingMuslims, Topbussey, rat_boy_sam, MultipleStabWounds, puncho, MICK THE MAG, EdgarBriggs, FantasticMrFucks, laba, Punch Drunk, Akin, bobbycov, Jesus-H-Christ, CallMeSir, Quadraplegicyetstilltyping, chappy7749, Spudrifle, shitguy, Deeps, CarlosDiablo, Martino231, boombyebye, tintin3000, immortalmaniac, Spurifle, coalition_cameron, BenBen, closetstr8, RodneyMyers, appy2be, suckplease, bloodyhellstefan, b3llend, Fusckdat, leisuresuitlee, jack the gripper, 8ace, drinkcelot, STM, DohertysDealer, henchboy, woolard, neekola, intershitty, simonlomas, emptyhead, ChickenShagger, WWMEDan, sick.fucker, pogo, deeezNI, GCG, djfishstik, prettyfly86, The crossbow cannibal, trampface, TheRizzler, kamsy123, Flacid7, El Twig, Chocosaurus, nailedon, poindexter, juniarrr, Daft Kaughn, anglebiter

8581484R00092

Printed in Great Britain
by Amazon.co.uk, Ltd.,
Marston Gate.